For Terry

From Jerry

FARM TRACTORS

A LIVING HISTORY

RANDY LEFFINGWELL

Motorbooks International
Publishers & Wholesalers

This book is dedicated to Dr. Reynold M. Wik, Oakland, California

Dr. Wik is Professor Emeritas of American History at Mills College, Oakland, California, from which he retired in 1975. He returned then to his undergraduate alma mater and began a new career as Professor of American History at Sioux Falls College, Sioux Falls, South Dakota. He retired from there in 1985.

Dr. Wik earned his PhD in American History from the University of Minnesota in 1949. His thesis became the first of three books published during his career, Steam Power on the American Farm, *printed in 1953. He has also authored* Henry Ford & Grass-roots American, *published in 1972 and* Benjamin Holt & Caterpillar Tracks & Combines, *published in 1984. In addition, he has written and had published more than 45 articles, making him one of the most significant and important historians of mechanized agriculture in North America.*

First published in 1995 by Motorbooks International Publishers & Wholesalers, PO Box 2, 729 Prospect Avenue, Osceola, WI 54020 USA

Printed in China

Library of Congress Cataloging-in-Publication Data
Leffingwell, Randy
Farm tractors : a living history / Randy Leffingwell.
p. cm.
Includes index.
ISBN 0-7603-0030-5
1. Farm tractors—Design and construction—History. I. Title.
TL233.L422 1995 95-5976
629.225—dc20

On the front cover: The Cockshutt Farm Equipment company was located in Brantford, Ontario, outside Toronto. In 1948, Cockshutt introduced its stylish Model 30, its appearance created by architectural designer Charlie Brooks. Cockshutt sold the tractor in the United States through the Co-operative Manufacturing Co. in Michigan as the Model E-3 and through other outlets, such as the Gambles department store chain as the Farmcrest Model 30. This four-cylinder Buda-engined tractor was restored and is owned by Raynard and Ruth Schmidt of Vail, Iowa.

On the frontispiece: This sulky plow is produced by Pioneer Equipment, Inc., of Dalton, Ohio, in the heart of a large Amish and Mennonite population. Pioneer plows are available in either left or right hand models of 12, 14, or 16in width. Hitches could be configured for two, three, or four horse teams. The plow weighs 440lb.

On the title page: A Fordson equipped with a home-built cab pulling a Ferguson-Sherman two-bottom plow. The tractor is owned by Palmer Fossum.

On the back cover: Top: The very first Model B produced, serial number B1000, owned by Walter Keller of Kaukauna, Wisconsin. Bottom: Farmall F-30 owned by Ray Pollock of Vail, Iowa.

Table of Contents

Acknowledgments

I AM VERY GRATEFUL TO THE COUNTLESS TRACTOR COLLECTORS, historians and enthusiasts in the United States and Canada for their boundless cooperation. In particular, I owe sincere thanks to the following individuals for their generous help in producing this book.

Mike Altman, Wesley, Iowa; Frank and Evelyn Bettencourt, Vernalis, California; the late Donald "Tiny" and Alice Blom, Manilla, Iowa; Paul Brecheisen, Helena, Ohio; Jerry and Alma Clark, Ceres, California; Rob W. Collins, Laoma, Wisconsin; Don and Patty Dougherty, Colfax, California; Paul, Ray and Willard Ehlinger, Wabeno, Wisconsin; Dwight and Katy Emstrom, Galesburg, Illinois; Ray and Dorothy Errett, Harlan, Iowa; Palmer and Harriett Fossum, Northfield, Minnesota; Edith Heidrick, Woodland, California; Walter and Lois Keller, Kaukauna, Wisconsin; and Bruce and Judy Keller, Brillion, Wisconsin; Paul Kirstein, Clarion, Iowa; Lester Larsen, Lincoln, Nebraska; Lester, Kenny and Harland Layher, Wood River, Nebraska; Larry and Melanie Maasdam, Clarion, Iowa; Clyde and Jeanette McCollough, Vail, Iowa; Jerry Mez, Avoca, Iowa; Roger Mohr, Vail, Iowa; Rodney Ott, Hilbert, Wisconsin; Gene Pionek, Wabeno, Wisconsin; Bob and Mary Pollock, Denison, Iowa; Raymond and Dorothy Pollock, Vail, Iowa; Henry Roskilly, Tavistock, Devon, England; Carlton Sather, Northfield, Minnesota; Randy and Monica Sawyers, Shelby, Iowa; Eugene F. Schmidt, Bluffton, Ohio; Raynard and Ruth Schmidt, Vail, Iowa; Wes, Bonnie and Scott Stoelk, Westside, Iowa; and Kermit Wilke, Wilcox, Nebraska.

In addition, my thanks goes, once again, to Lorry Dunning, Historical Consultant, Davis, California, for his tireless and speedy help.

I am grateful also to the Department of Special Collections, University of California, Davis, Library, and to its director, John Skarstad, for his continued support and assistance.

My sincere thanks go to Ms. Kim Kapin, General Manager, and Jim Yates, Director of Marketing of A&I Color Labs, Hollywood, California, for their constant critical care and watchful handling of all of my Kodachrome.

Finally, I am extremely indebted to Larry Armstrong, Director of Photography, Terry Schwadron, Assistant Managing Editor and Shelby Coffey III, Editor, *Los Angeles Times* for granting me the leave of absence during which time I worked on this project.

Randy Leffingwell
Los Angeles, California

333
MASSEY-HARRIS

Twentieth Century Entertainment

In a farm field one mile south and just off as far west of Exit 40 on Interstate 80 near Avoca in western Iowa, a small group of people waited impatiently for dark. It was just after Labor Day, a time of year when the sun settles to the ground at almost 275° by the compass and takes until nearly 8:50 p.m. to get there.

A stiff breeze had come up about 6 p.m., and some of the people wondered what effect it might have on the evening's activities. The wind blew hard out of the south at a steady 15–20mph. The sky filled with flat, gray-bottomed clouds that looked as though they had been scraped along the earth. The clouds were soiled and filed flat on the bottom, with billowing tops inflating upwards. Out at the horizon, though, the sky remained clear and blue. A few people looked to the north, concerned about the consequences of what was to come after dark.

The corn would be okay, they agreed, because it was still moist. The nearest house was a half mile beyond the corn, safely out of harm's way. The grass underneath their feet was dry, but rain during the week left everything too green to burn.

A pickup truck arrived loaded with nine Danish modern brown-stained wood chairs. The sagging foam cushions were covered in seventies knobby tweed. Folding metal chairs filled in the corners of the truck bed. Unloading it was like trying to remove one coat hanger from a bundle. Half the load came up at one tug; men joined in to untangle and unload. The chairs were set up in a diagonal line, slightly to the north and about 20ft east of the 1913 Russell 20hp steam traction engine that stood gently coughing at idle. A thin string of gray smoke rose from its stack. Abruptly cut off by the wind, it whipped to the north.

In the increasing gloom, women gathered children and flashlights. It would be too dark to see the way to cars or campers when they left. In the growing shadows forms moved, burdened with thermos bottles and six-packs of sodas or beer. The crowd grew in modest numbers. They were mostly friends of those participating in the threshing bee that had gone on all day, invited guests of the hosts of the evening.

"Will they still do it? Even with this wind?"

In answer, the Russell cracked the dusk with a long blast of its steam whistle. Randy Sawyers rolled his wrist on and off the cord, playing the single-note whistle like a Wurlitzer theater organ. Still, it was not yet fully dark.

There was activity around the Russell. Faceless figures moved at the front and rear. A hopper of kindling, wood shavings, and sawdust had been moved in the afternoon to a position near the back of the steam engine. Seventy feet forward was a low windmill, anchored to the ground with circus tent stakes. Its four paddles, each 2ft square, were meant to fight the wind even on calm days. It was loosely connected by a canvas belt to a large pulley wheel on the Russell. These devices were used to give a measure of an engine's performance. Knowing the diameters of the tractor and windmill pulleys and using a hand-held tachometer pressed against the windmill axle hub to count the revolutions, it was possible through a few simple calculations to determine "belt pulley horsepower."

But tonight, no one was counting.

Raleigh Woltmann reached up a gloved hand. He opened the front access door of the steamer's long, horizontal firebox. A volcanic glow lit his face. It was fully dark at last. The stars and moon were obscured by the cover blown in from Kansas.

Flashlights went on. Pools of light jiggled across the field toward cars. Doors opened and parents yelled to children to come put on sweaters and jackets to guard against a chilly south wind that made the night cool for early September. Feet shuffled through the grass to and from the Danish modern seating group. People returned, bundled in warmer clothes.

Sawyers opened the throttle on the Russell and, downwind, the windmill began to turn. It made white noise and tried to force back the low-pressure front moving in overhead. Woltmann swung the door open, and 5ft above him a few sparks shot out of the broad, trumpet-belled stack. The glowing cinders went up and quickly arced to the north. Sawyers opened more throttle, and a few more sparks shot like tracer rounds into the night to chase the others.

"Don't get excited folks," Woltmann yelled over the roar of the winds of God and Russell. "That's just the ashes inside the firebox. We haven't begun yet."

Sawyers opened the throttle to near full power. The chuffing sounded like the soundtrack from a railroad chase movie. The Russell, glowing from the front, turned orange at the rear as Sawyers checked its fire. The large machine at full speed, outlined in its own glow, ran evenly; it rested rock steady as though cemented to the ground.

Then Sawyers began. He shoveled a scoop of wood shavings into the fire door and Woltmann's face flashed white. A vesuvian molten stream of fire roared past the boiler tubes and curved like a liquid up into the stack. A column of yellow-orange streamers wound madly up into the sky, caught the wind, and rolled north toward the interstate a mile away.

Another scoop and another and another loaded up the firebox with flash fluff. A deep moan slipped out the front door past Woltmann. The light inside the Russell's round belly glared white. It cast Woltmann's shadow on the ground downhill toward the windmill and beyond, all the way to the corn.

Errant tracers, fallen out of the jet stream, glided into the turmoil of the windmill and were spun back into the air or down into the ground, or else off on wildly skewed trails of their own making.

The crowd in the Danish modern gallery longed out loud for popcorn. And they wondered more softly if city-folk got this much enjoyment out of Fourth of July firecrackers. Scoop after scoop of sawdust and wood chips went into the white heat and streamed out the black stack as the tractor labored on the belt, turning the windmill blades into blurs in the dark.

Interstate travelers pass this spot a mile to the north and are usually greeted with a six-mile stretch of seamless darkness to the south. Tonight, traffic in both directions was slowed by the spectacle. The fiery liquid orange spout was hurled 50ft up by the Russell's draft and roar and carried 100 yards downwind, like fireworks trailing off into the acrid smoke.

For another twenty minutes Sawyers and Woltmann played the Russell. One heaved shovels full of wood shards into the fire. The other controlled the draft and that sound, that deep bass moan of the draft, playing the front door like the wind instrument it was. For twenty minutes, traffic a mile away slowed as it crossed America and wondered if what it saw was real or just a product of road weariness.

When the gusts were interrupted by a lull, sparks soared like aerial skyrockets and fell back on themselves like the best of fireworks. Then the wind would pick up, and the orange geyser would sweep away in a tall flaming wall, heading toward the amazement of confused viewers, families, and truckers pulled to the shoulders along Interstate 80.

Then it was over. The last few weak fireflies turned tail and flamed off. Or they got tripped up and spun around by the windmill. A cheer and a round of applause went up. It was almost as loud and boisterous as any New York City or San Francisco field of spectators rising in praise of the Independence Day fireworks display.

Flashlights went on, and families drifted back to their cars or over to their campers. The chairs went back into the pickup bed. Sawyers and Woltmann moved around, shutting down the Russell for the night. The hellish fire had emptied the firebox, but the head of steam in the boiler would take longer to calm down.

Along the interstate, traffic began to move again. A huge semitrailer, visible even from the hillside, flashed its orange trailer lights rapidly.

"What do you suppose they all thought this was?" someone asked in the dark.

A long whoosh of steam bled off the boiler. Sawyers ripped two short and one long blast through the whistle into the night. It was the signal that steam work had finished.

"A field fire," a voice said matter-of-factly, hefting a Danish modern back into the pickup.

"Naw, fire wasn't movin'," said a voice farther away. "Prob'ly more likely a barn fire!" the voice offered.

"Too small," a woman replied. "And barns don't shoot up sparks from only one place."

"A volcano?" a younger voice spoke. Older voices laughed. "Well, it could be," the younger voice defended itself. "Mount St. Helens shot flames in the air."

The memory of the orange column sweeping up out of the black night and curving to the north came back clearly. So did the deep heaving groan as the wind roared through the firebox and was sucked up the stack.

"It was just a sparks show," Randy Sawyers said, his voice aimed toward the younger one. "That's all it was."

In the deep blustery dark, the younger voice tried on other options. "Mount Saint Russell?" A woman nearby chuckled.

"Come on, silly. It's past your bedtime."

"I've got it," the young voice trailed off into the wind. "Krakatoa, Western Iowa..."

One advantage of historical study and antique restoration is that students and practitioners often can find pleasure and amusement in the objects and tasks that were once used purely for work. It is hard to imagine that the rancher in Alberta or farmer in Kansas who was fortunate enough to own a 20hp steam traction engine in the early part of this century would have fired it up for evening entertainment. The risks that those sparks—wind-driven up from Oklahoma or down from the Arctic Circle—would destroy a few thousand acres preclude taking the chance, even if the owner was disposed to the lightheartedness it evokes. The development of the farm tractor has progressed so far, however, that a "sparks show" for friends and neighbors is one of the likely tasks for a steamer. It is the same with horses. Farming with horses or mules at this end of the twentieth century is something done for religious reasons on farms that function to provide family livelihood. Or else they work on farms that serve as a diversion and a hobby for their owners. When horses were no longer beasts of agricultural burden or urban commerce, riding them became a pleasure activity. The techniques of breeding draft horses for strength were modified to the big business of breeding race horses for speed.

The history of agriculture progressed for thousands of years with oxen, horses, and mules before steam was tamed. A few decades later, gasoline replaced steam. Barely two more decades passed before liquefied petroleum gases were brought under control, and at nearly the same time, Dr. Rudolf Diesel's engines were introduced. Within four more decades, diesel power's strength and reliability made every other fuel source obsolete.

What uses will Ford's articulated four-wheel-drive tractors or Caterpillar's rubber-tracked Challengers serve in another half century? Will they do more than fill collectors' sheds and museums? What will have replaced them in daily use? It is entertaining to speculate as to what nostalgic purposes their replacements will be put in the year 2100.

Chapter One

Horse Farming Draws to a Close

Taking Power Off the Hoof

Otto von Guericke launched the world into self-propelled motion roughly 350 years ago in Germany. While it would take nearly another 200 years for machines derived from his discoveries to move from their own power, it was the results of his work that encouraged the possibilities.

Von Guericke was aware of the axiom that nature abhors a vacuum. He theorized that there was no air in outer space, because if there was, its friction would have slowed the travel of planets and stars. To satisfy his curiosity, he set out to create a vacuum. The fifty-year-old philosopher took a hollow brass sphere and something like a bicycle pump to suck the air *out* of the sphere. He watched his sphere, and even though he imagined what might happen, he was shocked when it did. After most of the air had been pumped out, the sphere crumpled in on itself.

Von Guericke had discovered atmospheric pressure, an element that would prove crucial to the functioning of internal-combustion engines. He continued experimenting with larger pumps and spheres. His pump consisted of a piston and connecting rod inside a cylinder with valves. At one end of the closed pump was the sphere; at the other, the connecting rod protruded through a sealed cap to a handle. Using this kind of simple "engine," he engaged his own arm muscles as the fuel for the driving force to pull out the pump handle. Releasing the handle at the top of its pull away from the sphere, he watched as the connecting shaft was pulled back into the cylinder, by itself. This result was energy without human, wind, or water power. Of course, the vacuum—the low air pressure—created inside the sphere was simply pulling back its own air from inside the pump. The piston, pulled up by von Guericke, was pulled back by the vacuum.

▲*The Phoenix Log Hauler tender held about 315gal with another 400–450gal in the tank. The steam operated two 6.5x8in compound cylinders on each side, producing a total of 100hp. This power was delivered equally by a single throttle-valve to all four cylinders. Tracks were iron, with twenty-nine pads per side, moving on Cletrac-like track-rollers. Track gauge was 65in.*

▸*Paul Ehlinger watches the stack blow above him. This 1909 Phoenix Log Hauler runs summer demonstrations in Wabeno, Wisconsin, where this and two other identical machines were owned by G.W. Jones Lumber. This machine, #79, was the lumber mill yard tractor. The only steering was accomplished by this wheel; there were no track brakes or clutches; a main-drive clutch stopped or engaged forward or rearward motion.*

A young Dutch physicist, Christiaan Huygens, lived in Paris at this time, around 1650. Huygens and his younger French assistant, Denis Papin, were both born and raised during the Thirty Years War, a conflict that introduced western civilization to gunpowder. Huygens was a pacifist with an imagination. He had invented the pendulum clock and perfected the telescope.

Envisioning French King Louis XIV's cannons as a kind of open-ended air pump of the type von Guericke had experimented with, Huygens imagined the cannonball as a surrogate piston. He reasoned that if gunpowder was placed below the cannonball in a sealed cannon tube and the gunpowder was ignited, then at the top of the sealed tube, the air compressed by the rising ball—Louis XIV's piston—would force it back down. Remarkably, neither Huygens nor Papin were killed during their experiments. The efforts proved Huygens correct. For a grander version of his experiment, his piston was fixed to a rod through the cannon's sealed end, onto which a rope was then attached. In a demonstration for the French government, Huygens lit the fuse. The explosion inside the tube raised the piston. This moved the rope and lifted a platform loaded with men. It was an internal-combustion engine that produced heat. It had now put that heat energy to work.

But fresh gunpowder could not be continuously injected into a hot cylinder without disastrous results. Papin realized that steam made in the cylinder could force the piston away as well, compressing the air at the other end. When the steam cooled, the piston returned. But Papin's imagination didn't extend far enough. He did not conceive of an outside source of steam that was fed continuously into the cylinder and that would be bled off on the piston's return. Even when the idea came to him, Papin

was plagued by pipes that leaked, seals that failed against the pressure, and seventeenth century technology that was unable to cast a perfectly round cylinder.

The lack of perfect cylinders plagued Thomas Newcomen in Devonshire, England, as well. For something like a decade, from around 1698 probably until sometime in 1708, he and his assistant, John Calley, labored to produce a pump to remove water flooding the coal mines. A Londoner, Thomas Savery, a Newcomen contemporary, had done work with steam that he heated and condensed in two separate chambers to produce a nearly continuous suction pressure in hopes of withdrawing water from great depths out of the mines. Pipes fitted with one-way valves extended down into the mine water and up out the top to a run-off. But Savery's system required great boiler pressure. His soldered seams occasionally melted from the heat generated by the boiler fire, and the steam and condensed water had to be vented by hand valves operated by an attendant usually stationed in the middle of the mine-shaft. Savery's pumps were estimated

▾The left front ski of the Phoenix Log Hauler emerges from the bleed-off of a full head of steam. The Phoenix Lumber Company of Eau Claire, Wisconsin, licensed the production of this example and more than sixty others from lumberman/ inventor Alvin Lombard of Maine. Lombard and Phoenix eventually produced about 215 of these machines, used across the northern United States and into Canada. Lombard later ended up in a furious patent dispute with Caterpillar inventor Ben Holt over crawler-tractor design.

to be successful at sucking up water as much as 150ft. Little evidence exists, however, that they did better than 20ft. He gave up all efforts at mine pumps after 1705.

Newcomen may or may not have known of Savery's work. Records of Newcomen's early life do not exist. It is 160mi from Devon to London, and in the seventeenth century, news of the success or failures of inventions traveled slowly. It is more likely that the stories of Papin's work were known widely. Their coincidental developments were simply a case where several inventors, obsessed by the same need, set the same goals and arrived at similar conclusions.

Newcomen understood that the condensation of the steam in his cylinder drew the piston pump back as the pressure inside sought to equal the atmospheric pressure outside. He realized that relying on the outside air to cool his cylinder slowed his engine's work to an imperceptible pace. He first tried cooling the cylinder by pouring cold water over the outside walls. Then he tried to jacket the cylinder and control the cooling flow surrounding it. But this proved to be barely any improvement over air cooling. Then one day, one of Newcomen's soldered repairs in his cylinder gave way. A tiny hole allowed cold water to stream rapidly into the cylinder. This cooled the vapor quickly. The connecting rod had been attached to a balance beam and to a weight, duplicating on a smaller scale the work achieved by Huygens' cylinder. The accidental cold-water injection condensed Newcomen's steam so fast and so forcefully that the chain broke. The piston crushed the bot-

▲*The coldest job in North America was reputed to be that of tillerman on the Lombard or Phoenix in a Maine, Ontario, or Wisconsin winter. The Log Hauler was capable of hauling out sleighs loaded with a dozen or more 15–16ft tree sections at speeds of 6–8mph. But all the heat was behind the tillerman, who sat out in the elements. In Maine, there were stories of putting an outhouse on the platform around the tillerman and the assistant.*

tom of the cylinder and the lid of the boiler as well.

Thomas Newcomen, an ironmonger by trade, a metal-craftsman in fact, had succeeded in making a rapid-acting steam engine. However, it had acted only for one cycle. Hand-operated valves had been fitted to the top of the boiler to allow fresh cold water in to replace the quantity lost to steam. It was now Newcomen's chore to conjure a method of making these valves fast-acting and, indeed, self-activating, if this engine was ever to be capable of continuous work.

John Farey, an architect and engineer in the early 1700s, witnessed a production Newcomen engine, and his "Treatise On the Steam Engine," is quoted in R. L. T. Rolt's 1963 book, *Thomas Newcomen: The Prehistory of the Steam Engine*. "At first the valves were opened and shut by hand," Farey observed, "and required the most exact and unremitting care of the attendant to perform those operations at the precise moment; the least neglect or inadvertence might be ruinous to the machine, by beating out the bottom of the cylinder, or allowing the piston to be drawn wholly out of it."

Dr. William Stukeley, a London physician, visited a Newcomen pump installation in Whitehaven, England, in 1725 and described its workings. Rolt quoted from Stukeley's notes. "It creates a vacuum by first rarefying the air with hot steam, then condenses it suddenly by cold water," Stukeley wrote, "whense [*sic*] a piston is drawn up and down alternately, at one end of the beam: this actuates a pump at the other end, which, let down into the works, draws the water out: it makes about fourteen strokes a minute."

According to Rolt, an engineer named Henry Beighton invented a linkage that he had installed on a Newcomen-style pump in 1718. The linkage ran from the pump's balance beam to the valves and opened and shut each of them in time to the action of the pump and the steam boiler. It was, in effect, one of the earliest valve rocker-arms, establishing an engine mechanism that has been in use ever since. With Beighton's improvement, Newcomen's steam pump became a reliable steam engine, ready for the next step in its development. This would translate the vertical shaft movement to rotary motion.

Because the stroke length of the Newcomen engine varied with the amount of steam admitted to or expelled from the cylinder, Newcomen's contemporaries failed to consider that a crankshaft and flywheel might serve to even out the stroke and average out the production of power. Instead, they felt that its irregular stroke prohibited the engine from becoming a rotating power source. It was not until 1763 that Joseph Oxley of Northumberland patented a ratchet device that prevented the crankshaft from turning backwards if the steam pressure dipped for any period of time. Yet, Oxley's ratchet device was flawed, as were those that followed during the next several years.

James Watt, a Scottish engineer and scientist, made the improvements that turned Newcomen's beam engine into a practical machine that would fit many more applications. His first idea, patented in 1769, separated the condenser function from the piston cylinder. This meant that the cylinder could remain near steam heat all the time. The condenser, shot with cold water, sucked the steam out of the cylinder, pulling the piston down

▴*The Log Hauler stands 124in high, 73in wide, and it's 228in long overall. It was used by G.W. Jones Lumber Co. in Wabeno until 1929 and then sold to the City of Wabeno, Wisconsin, in 1935. It required a steam engineer, fireman, tillerman, and assistant to operate it. These days, volunteers such as certified steam engineer Rob Collins of Laona, Wisconsin, and tillerman Paul Ehlinger make do with hands full.*

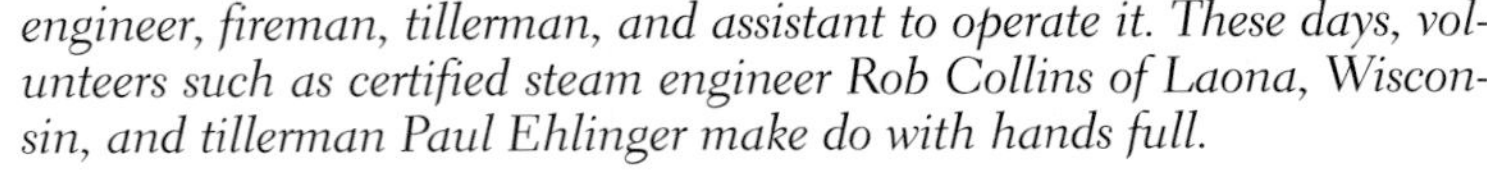

to the bottom of the cylinder. Then steam could be immediately injected into the hot cylinder chamber to raise the piston again. This increased the number of cycles possible per minute and decreased substantially the amount of fuel burned in heating steam for the cylinder.

On a suggestion from his assistant, William Murdock, Watt attached his piston to a crankshaft in order to convert the reciprocal piston movement into rotation. But an ex-employee stole that idea and patented it first, forcing Watt to adapt. He adopted a sun-and-planet gear system and used that until 1794, when the crankshaft patent entered public domain.

With both the sun-and-planet gear system (where the connecting rod ended in a geared wheel that rotated around a geared center shaft) and the crankshaft, it was possible to add a flywheel. This evened out the action of the piston in the cylinder, making it more useful and manageable for other tasks. Perfection of the duplex engine—essentially two pistons working within the same cylinder, one always being in compression stroke—followed quickly.

Probably the first attempt at putting to work the inventions

◂*The Log Hauler, patented May 21, 1901, operated as a curious mix of steam traction engine and steam locomotive. It had no compressor to operate air brakes as on a locomotive. Neither did it have a clutch as found on some steam traction engines. Friction on ice or snow from the load—-sometimes as much as 100,000 board feet on as many as twenty-five 12ft-wide sleighs behind it—-stopped it effectively. For the demonstrations each summer, the front skis are replaced with steel wheels.*

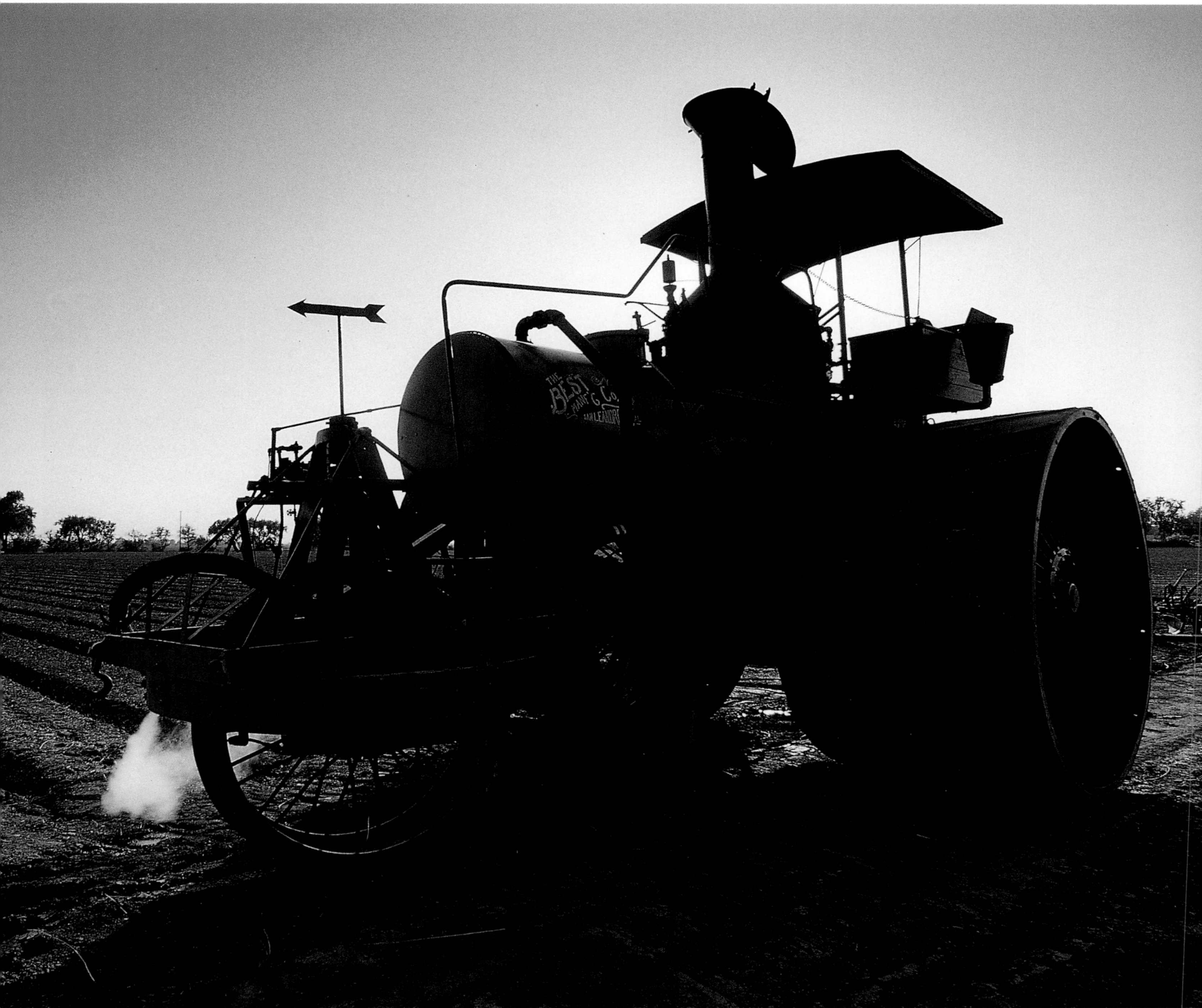

▲*Daniel Best's big 110hp steamers were available either as 28ft long freight haulers or like this 22ft long agricultural version. The shorter, more maneuverable agricultural models operated on round drive wheels 8ft in diameter and 5ft wide. Wood or metal extensions sometimes added another 12ft to wheel width on each side to keep the eleven-ton tractors from sinking into soft soil. This 1904 steamer is owned by Mrs. Edith Heidrick of Woodland, California.*

of Newcomen and Watt appeared in railroad locomotives. The first self-propelled road vehicle was Nicolas Cugnot's Steam Road Wagon, completed in 1769. But the first known agricultural application of a steam traction engine—that is, an engine that could haul itself and possibly other vehicles as its normal function—came from an English locomotive builder, E. B. Wilson & Co., at the Railway Foundry in Leeds. Known as the "Farmer's Engine," it was designed in 1849 by Wilson & Co.'s chief designer Robert Willis.

The Farmer's Engine was a two-cylinder simple engine, with a 6.25x10.0in bore and stroke. According to Ronald H. Clark in his 1960 book, *The Development of the English Traction Engine*, the Wilson Farmer's Engine worked for several weeks towing and operating a small threshing machine northeast of London. The horizontal coal boiler operated at 45psi yet produced barely 4.3hp. It burned 61lb of coal per hour and evaporated 41gal/hr. Yet with its two-speed gearing, it was capable of 12mph on level ground. It dispensed with horses completely. It was self-steering and self-propelled, the two pistons operating tractor-length connecting rods attached to a crankshaft and by gears attached to the rear driving axle.

From 1857 through 1862, John Smith, a farmer, engineer, and machinist in central England, produced half-a-dozen chain-driven traction engines. Smith mounted his boilers so they could be pivoted, raised, or lowered from the rear, to keep the boiler level while climbing or descending. At normal working pressure of

▲**M***elanie Maasdam, of Clarion, Iowa, works her two Belgians behind a Jenny Lind cultivator. On the left, Jane, is a 1,750lb eleven-year old mare, and on the right is Mary, an 1,800lb ten-year old mare. A rule of thumb in horse farming is to use the larger horse on the right.*

▲**N***eighbor Paul Kirstein rides a John Deere cultivator behind Melanie Maasdam's Belgians. Kirstein grew up on an eighty-acre farm that used horses well into the early sixties. He got back into it as a hobby. In plowing or cultivating, he recalled, "It was peaceful. All you heard was the earth cracking and the horses' hooves clodding."*

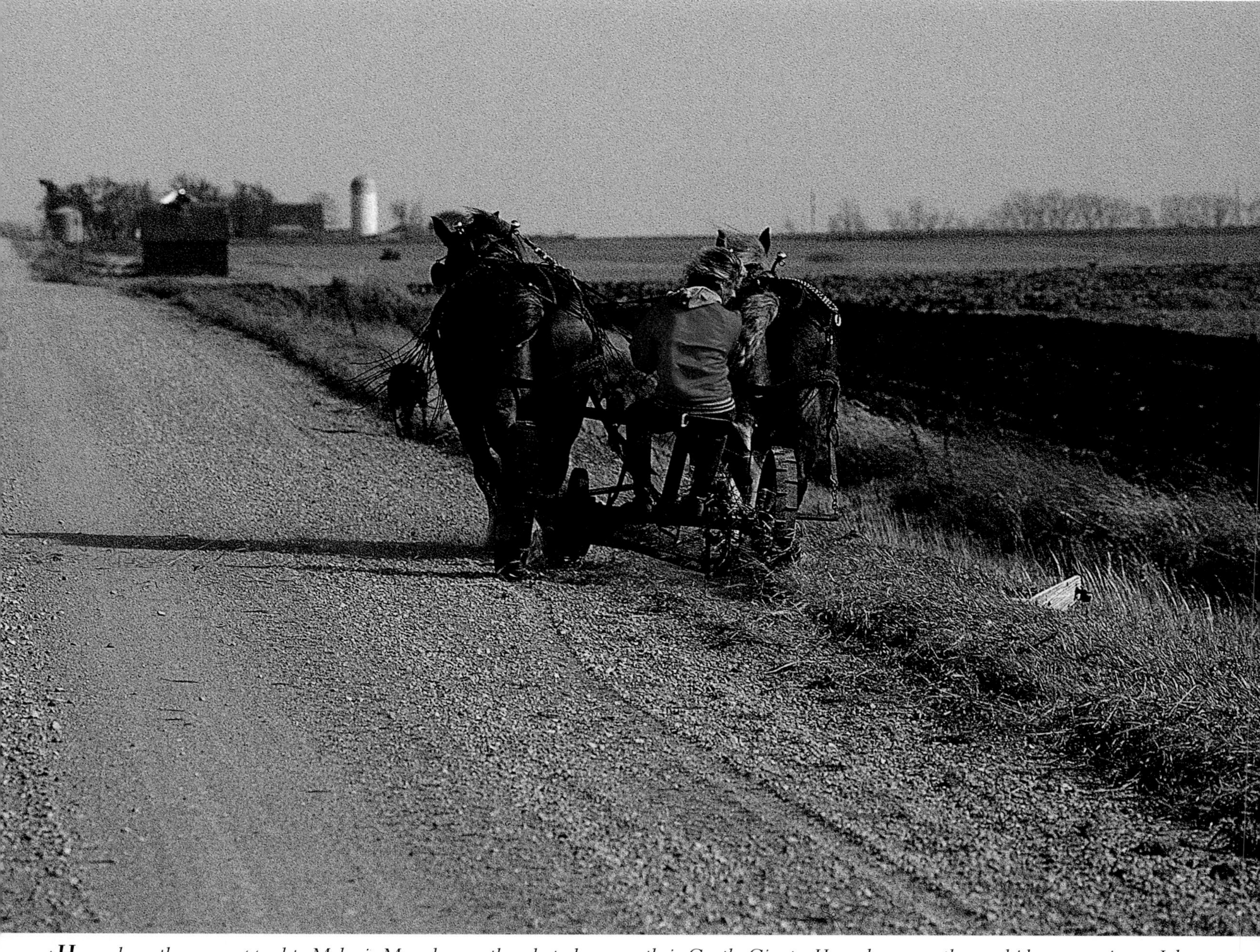

▲*Horses have the same appeal to Melanie Maasdam as they do to her friend, Paul Kirstein. Melanie and husband Larry refer to the horses as their Gentle Giants. Here she mows the roadside grass using a John Deere No. 3 horse-drawn mower.*

60psi, Smith's traction engines produced 10hp. Smith learned his engineering skills working for John Fowler & Company of Leeds.

Fowler produced railroad locomotives, and the configuration of Smith's and later of Fowler's own steam traction engines benefited from their experiences. Fowler's traction engine in 1868, designed by David Greig, used a single duplex 6.5x12in cylinder and even drove all four wheels. The Fowler, Smith, and Wilson engines were all "undermounted"; that is, the engines' cylinders and flywheels were below the boilers.

But many other makers placed their cylinders on top of the boiler, and self-propulsion was accomplished through chains from the "overmounted" crankshaft to the large rear drive wheels. A number of these "portable" engines still relied on horses for steering, but history suggests that the horses often did more than steer.

"The underlying idea of making these heavy engines self moving," Clark wrote, "was to spare the horses much killing labour. I have had it from several sources that many fine animals have been strained and later necessarily destroyed as a result of getting bogged portables out of awkward places."

At the same time as E. B. Wilson's Farmer's Engine in England in 1849, a Philadelphian, A. L. Archanbault, introduced his Forty-Niner series for 4, 10, and 30hp horse-drawn portables. In 1850, Gideon Morgan of Calhoun, Tennessee, received a patent for improvements to a track-type tractor wheel substitute. This suggests that a crawler or tracklayer-style steamer existed at least in design before that time.

The first steam traction crawler in England was designed by Richard Bach of Birmingham in 1854. At the rear of one of his 8hp portable engines, he used the "Boydell's Patent Endless Railway," a kind of articulated plank arrangement that James Boydell first patented in 1846. William Tuxford produced several varieties of vertical boiler-equipped Boydell crawlers, and Charles Burrell produced many models of overmounted, horizontal boilers, complete with front- and rear-planked wheels, the huge rears being enclosed in sheet metal like an orchard tractor from a century later. Both Tuxford and Burrell Boydell-style steam traction engines were shipped as far away as Egypt and Brazil.

This was a morning when the operators could sleep in. Randy Sawyers of Council Bluffs, Iowa, brings the Russell out for demonstrations and for a threshing bee in Avoca, Iowa, each September. Threshing has become entertainment rather than work, so everything waits till after sunup to begin.

The technology and ideas crossed the Atlantic with the machines. In his 1976 book, *Encyclopedia of American Steam Traction Engines*, C. H. Wendel chronicled the history. In 1854, Henry Ames in Oswego, New York, founded one of the first factories in North America to build portable steamers. A year later, Obed Hussey produced his first steam plow in Baltimore, Maryland, and the race was on. Blandy Steam Engine Works in Zanesville, Ohio, offered portable engines from 3hp to 35hp, ranging in price from $300 to $2,300. Wheeler & Melick Co. in Albany, New York, produced 6, 8 and 10hp portables, operating at up to 200psi in 1877. But by then, companies such as the American Engine Company in Jersey City, New Jersey, had their first traction engines in production for two years. Henry Ames produced his first one in 1885.

By 1900, there were at least sixty-eight companies that had produced and sold steam traction engines in North America (although many had already gone out of business by that time). Seventeen of them were in Ohio alone. Twelve more were located in New York while five were established in Ontario.

Engineering features and developments ranged as far and wide as manufacturer locations. As early as 1871, D. D. Williamson in New York City produced a vertical boiler traction engine that was mounted on hard rubber tires. The Scottish inventor, R. W. Thompson, had developed the inflatable pneumatic tire in the late 1860s . Williamson contracted with Grant's Locomotive Works across the Hudson River in New Jersey, and fifty rubber-tired steamers were built.

The Lansing Iron and Engine Works, founded in Lansing, Michigan, in 1876 and out of business by about 1898, produced the 12hp Lansing Double Traction engine, a four-wheel-drive overmounted steamer. A marvelous jumble of chains drove both the solid front axle (that pivoted inside its large sprocket to turn) and the rear wheels.

Sawyer & Massey in Hamilton, Ontario, became Canadian agents for the English Aveling & Porter steam traction engines in 1887. A change was soon made to the locomotive-type boiler that would burn wood, coal, or straw. Throughout the 1890s, Sawyer & Massey produced traction engines ranging from 13hp up to 35hp. Within two decades, the company was producing 25 to 76hp compound engines, machines powerful enough to break sod in Alberta or operate sawmills in British Columbia.

In Massillon, Ohio, three brothers formed C. M. Russell & Co. as a general carpentry business. They quickly expanded into producing railroad cars and threshing machines, and, by the mid-1880s, portable 6hp steam engines. Almost immediately, the Russells had devised geared transmissions and chain-and-roller steering and produced 6hp and 10hp steam traction engines.

Russell followed common practice as technology and development continued around the world. The company overmounted the engines, placing cylinders up front to lessen the distance the steam traveled. This positioned the crankshaft above the center of the boiler, providing the minimum distance for gears to get power to the rear drive wheels. Russell tractors used a friction clutch and were equipped with two forward speeds and a reverse gear. Power quickly increased, and before 1900, Russell offered tractors with up to 16hp. Russell used single-cylinder configurations even for the 30hp engines of the early 1920s. The company introduced its 20hp model in 1912. For purposes of rigidity, the engine cylinder, steam chest, slide housing, and half the crankcase box were cast in a single piece, mounted atop the boiler. This was necessary since the largest Russell produced 67hp off the crankshaft-driven belt pulley. By the time the company

quit manufacturing steam traction engines, power had increased to 150hp, used more for road freight hauling than agricultural purposes.

In California, Dan Best and Ben Holt had the market largely to themselves because of the high cost of transporting traction engines around the Rocky Mountains. Soil conditions in the central California valleys necessitated huge wheel extensions, some as much as 26ft on a side. These were required to keep the heavy 110hp Best and Holt steamers on top of the peat bogs or sandy soils that California farmers had come to value. The developments of James Boydell with his planked wheels interested both Best and Holt very much.

Work by a Maine farmer and lumber mill owner, Alvin Lombard, attracted Holt and Best as well. Lombard had invent-

Belted up to the fan, the Russell could put out much more than its drawbar-rated 20hp. This model used an 8.25x12in simple engine. The universal boiler contained thirty-six of the 2.5in tubes; this was different from the standard models fitted with about fifty of the 2in diameter tubes. Belt horsepower was nearer to sixty-five.

ed a locomotive-type engine for use during the summer for plowing, but more important, during the winter as a log hauler. Front wheels were replaced by wooden skis, and the Log Hauler's crawler tracks provided unmatched traction. In one trip out of the Maine woods, Lombard pulled nearly 100,000 board feet of logs. The Phoenix Lumber Company in Eau Claire, Wisconsin, learned of Lombard's machines and bought one, and then negotiated the rights to manufacture them. Phoenix's Log Haulers used neither under- nor overmounted engines but instead fitted two cylinders vertically on either side of the long boiler. Worse, steering was accomplished by a tillerman seated outside on a bench mounted in front of the boiler. It was surely the coldest job imaginable. The 100hp engines were capable of phenomenal work over eastern and midwestern snow-covered logging roads. Phoenix eventually sold 200 of the Log Haulers, all with external steering.

Ben Holt learned of the Log Hauler's crawler tracks and adopted its technology to create his Caterpillars. Holt eventually built eight of the steam-powered crawlers, although both he and Daniel Best already had produced hundreds of wheel-type traction engines.

Huge steam traction engines worked well enough on farms of average size in the eastern and midwestern United States. They served even better on the vast ranches of the western states and provinces of Canada, breaking prehistoric sod for first planting. But in England, land was more scarce, and farms were much smaller. Even maneuvering a steamer with eight or twelve plows behind it required huge spaces, room that was better served in cultivation.

As early as 1800, patents were issued in England for frames carrying winding drums and cables or ropes to draw plows or cultivators across fields. By 1856, John Fowler & Co. had patented a system of cable-operated plows driven by a single steam traction engine and double rollers anchored to the ground on the opposite side of the field. This was first conceived as a way to plow wet ground to bury drainpipes. Version after version were tried, including placing the steamer on one bank of the field and a wheeled, movable windlass on the opposite bank. But each move took time. The cables had to be slacked, the anchors released, the windlass moved forward, and the anchors reset. By 1865, John Fowler had perfected a system using two of his engines, each fitted with a horizontal winding drum below the boiler. These were placed on opposite sides of the field, and while one played out fourteen-gauge steel cable, the other wound it up. A two-way plow was used so the furrows fell the same direction, and the two engines simply inched their way up the field headlands. Fowler sold not only plows but also cultivators and subsoilers to work this system, enabling his engines to perform work for which the steam traction engines were otherwise impossibly unsuited because of their size and weight.

But even with the enhanced efficiency that dozens of talented engineers and inventors obtained through Watt's rotary movement and his other improvements—slide valves for steam intake and exhaust and pressure gauges—the steam engine was immensely impractical. At its best, it produced only 4 percent thermal efficiency. That is the percentage of useful work an engine performs in comparison to the total energy content of the fuel consumed. Furthermore, it took as much as two hours to get one up to operating pressure. And it was dangerous: Leaks in pipes scalded operators; improperly at-

tended boilers exploded. The weight of the engines broke rural bridges, stranding the machines in sometimes irretrievable positions. The smoke from their fireboxes choked the air.

Still, with no alternative, operators from the time of James Watt would endure another one hundred years of dissatisfaction and experimentation before an alternative would appear. And it required an unrelated discovery in Pennsylvania in the 1850s to ensure that its replacement would succeed.

▸▸*The 6ft x 12ft canopy was a $50 option at the time these steamers were new. A small wood cab was offered as well, for about $150. Without water in the boiler or wood in the bins, the 20hp model weighed 20,800lb.*

RUSSELL
THE RUSSELL & COMPANY
BUILDERS
MASSILLON OHIO USA

THE BOSS
WHEN ORDERING REPAIRS
PLEASE MENTION
NUMBER OF THIS ENGINE

WHEN ORDERING REPAIRS
PLEASE MENTION
NUMBER OF THIS ENGINE
SOLD 1914 BY
CLARK IMPLIMENT CO.
COUNCIL BLUFFS IOWA

◂*The Russell Company was founded in Massillon, Ohio, in 1838 and was famous first for making railroad cars and steam shovels. Their first steam tractor, a 6hp self-propelled, self steering model, was introduced in 1887. Russell remained in business until 1927, producing steam traction engines as large as 150hp. This 1913 20hp model was restored and is owned by Randy Sawyers of Council Bluffs, Iowa.*

Chapter Two

Dawn of Internal Combustion

Taking the Next Step

The oil discovered under the eastern United States was first processed for lamp fuel in the mid-1800s. Ironically, as gas processing improved and steam power was fully domesticated another fifty years later, gas that flowed in the headlamps lit the roads at night for steam-powered automobiles. This was a true technological contradiction if ever there was one.

Physicists, chemists, inventors, tinkerers, and experimenters all understood heat engines well enough by 1850. In fact, they knew a century earlier that to replace steam required new thinking. The heat that expanded the air to force the piston to move the crank to spin the flywheel *must* be created inside the cylinder. Internal combustion would eliminate the boiler, the firebox, and the steam. If only they could bring the firebox inside the cylinder and create the steam pressure instantaneously, and repeatedly, then they would have a practical engine.

Processed coal produced gas that was piped into homes for illumination. This was not without its own problems, of course, but its potential for small engines was obvious. The great industrial revolution had begun to pay benefits. Steam-powered belt-driven lathes and tools, operated and patented by iron craftsmen like John Wilkinson of England, turned out not only exquisite decorative sword blades but also precise cylinders and true pipes. New processes improved the quality of metals, blending and hybridizing them for strength and longevity. In laboratories throughout Europe and North America, electric sparks became more controllable. And in book-lined libraries and classrooms, under the attentive gaze of enraptured students and assistants, mathematicians and theoreticians demonstrated a better understanding of just what happened when heat produced energy. The patent offices got very busy.

▲Bore and stroke was 7.5x9.0in. The giant Bear produced thirty drawbar and fifty belt pulley horsepower at 650rpm. The engine used a gear-driven oil pump to pressure-lubricate not only the crankshaft and cylinder walls but also the connecting rods and wrist pins. This was the third of nine ever produced, manufactured in late 1911, and it is owned and was restored by E.F. Schmidt of Bluffton, Ohio.

▸It was tractors like these that prompted agricultural journalists to call for more compact tractors. Its front wheel was actually a pair of 12x42in steel drums. The Bear measured 22ft long overall and stood 93.5in to the top of the exhaust. It was 99.5in wide and weighed 10.5 tons. Its four-cylinder 1,480ci engine was capable of pulling 8–10 14in plows. There was nothing small about the Wallis Bear.

In 1791, Englishman John Barber received a patent for his gas turbine engine. Historian Lyle Cummins wrote of Barber's work in his 1976 book, *Internal Fire*. The discoveries of Christiaan Huygens and Denis Papin suggested to Barber that other flammable substances besides gunpowder could be used to power his engine. If ignited in a closed cylinder, these materials could turn the resultant heat into work. Barber used coal gas, but unlike Watt's developments with rotary motion, Barber used the force of the exhausted combustion. He channeled it through a small opening. This was directed toward a turbine wheel that he geared to an output shaft. Cummins' thorough research failed to turn up any working examples of Barber's early turbine, but the historian offered an insight. From Barber's patent it was clear that he had already imagined that his managed exhaust stream had enough force to be used as its own form of propulsion. This hinted at, as Cummins wrote, the technology of the jet engine that would evolve some 140 years later.

Countless other efforts followed. Each advanced by inches the development of internal combustion of vaporized gas in a repetitive, reliable manner. Then, in Paris in 1860, Etienne Lenoir received a patent for his gasoline-burning engine with two opposed cylinders, similar to the duplex, or compound, engines of steamers. As one piston began its downstroke, it sucked in a gas/air mix that was immediately sparked, forcing the piston the rest of the way down. The flywheel's momentum brought the crank around. This brought the opposite piston down, forcing the other one up to blow out the exhaust. It was smooth and quiet, and it was as powerful and three times as fuel efficient as contemporary steam engines of equal output. By 1864, there were 130 of them running in Paris alone.

WALLIS BEAR
OWNERS

▲*The Wallis Tractor Company was located in Cleveland, Ohio at the time it produced the Bear. Founder H.M. Wallis was a relative of Jerome Increase Case and Wallis served for a time as president of J.I. Case Plow Works in Racine, Wisconsin, founded in 1876 to build plows (this was not the same company and had no relation to the J.I. Case Threshing Machine Company, also in Racine, except to guarantee confusion over use of Case's name). In 1919, Wallis Tractor Company merged with J.I. Case Plow Works. The Plow Works was bought by Massey-Harris in 1928 and the J.I. Case name alone was sold to J.I. Case Threshing Machine Company almost immediately. This cleared up the confusion.*

◄*The Wallis Tractor Company of Racine, Wisconsin, first showed the Bear in its 1902 catalogs. By 1914, Wallis was owned by J.I. Case Plow Works but in February, 1927, both were purchased by Massey-Harris Company, Ltd., of Toronto, Ontario, Canada. Tractor manufacture then continued at the J.I. Case Plow Works factory in Racine.*

In Cologne, Germany, in early 1862, Nicolaus Otto was a distracted thirty-year-old. Working as a salesman by day, Otto apprenticed himself to a machinist, and he worked nights on his own projects in his master's shop. He had his own ideas that were based on Lenoir's machine. The noise of his ideas kept the neighbors awake.

Experimenting first with alcohol, then with a variety of petroleum spirits, he fabricated a kind of vaporizing carburetor that heated alcohol and pumped it into a cylinder. He labored and struggled for years. His intention was to get away from a fuel

▸*The rear drive wheels were 30x84in. Despite being produced so early in the gasoline engine age, this was an extremely advanced tractor. It offered power steering, individual turning brakes, a spring-loaded clutch, an enclosed three-speed transmission, and an all-speed governor. Many of these features would not appear on other makes for decades.*

▴*Daniel Best produced crawler tractors he called Tracklayers. Steering was accomplished by a differential incorporating steering clutches that slowed the track inside the turn while speeding the track outside. As the dirt marks indicate, the tractor could turn nearly inside its own length using this type of steering.*

source that was fixed to a building. He knew that taking his fuel from the gas lines that provided heat and light for the building limited the usefulness of his ideas. And the noise of his labors continued to keep the neighbors awake. As he wrote in his first patent application, his ultimate goal was to produce an engine "to propel vehicles serviceably and easily along country roads, as well as prove useful for the purposes of small industry."

Patent denied.

The Royal Ministry of Commerce of the Kingdom of Prussia had already patented vaporizing carburetors; however, nothing in the ministry's rejection spoke of self-propelled, self-contained vehicles. Otto convinced his master, Michael Zons, to construct a Lenoir-type engine. Then Otto tinkered and puttered. He altered and modified. Still, he kept the neighbors awake, and almost by mistake, he discovered something significant.

Experimenting with his fuel-and-air mixture, he allowed

WALLIS' BEAR
OWNERS

▲The Best 25 tractor was produced from 1918 through 1920. The Model B engine was available without the tractor at a cost of $832 and was used in saw mills and to run harvesters. This Model B engine was Best's own design and produced 25hp at 800rpm, 12hp on the drawbar, and was capable of pulling 2500lb in low gear. This is a 1918 model.

▲*Best's Model 25 was the test model for what would become the Model 30 and 60. The 25s introduced an enclosed transmission and steering clutches. Previously, all this machinery had been exposed to outside dirt. In addition, the Model 25 was fitted with a gear-drive oil pump. The oil was pumped into a trough in the sump pan. As the crankshaft rotates, the connecting rod dipped into the trough and oil was splashed to where it was required.*

more of the mix to be sucked into his test cylinder than was usual. He wondered what would happen if he turned the flywheel back one more turn, to drop the piston as far down its travel as it would go. He reasoned that this would allow even more mixture into the cylinder. When he released the flywheel, the mixture ignited violently, and the flywheel rotated several more times on its own rather than just the usual one revolution he had achieved in all his previous attempts.

Back up the flywheel then. Let the fuel in. Release the flywheel. Spark, explosion, and several revolutions. And again. Until he knew he could repeat it every time. Until he began to imagine it running longer than just those several revolutions. What about running continuously?

So again he repeated the process, and then he concluded that he needed a new timing gear. What he had found was that the Lenoir design did not allow for the extra stroke that would let in the additional fuel that seemed to turn the engine crank more times.

Otto allowed a full downstroke of the piston to fill the cylinder and a full upstroke for compression, then let it spark! A full downstroke of combustion power was the result. Then it began again. His flywheel brought the piston back to the top, to push out the burned fuel, and then back down to suck in a fresh mixture. Confidently, he and Zons created a new engine. But this time, showing a greater faith in his own conclusions, he built

◂*Best used an Ensign-designed 1.5in carburetor and a Bosch or Splitdorf magneto on the Model B. The Model B engine was an in-line four-cylinder 4.625x5.25in engine with a total capacity of 302ci. This rare tractor is owned by Jerry Clark of Ceres, California.*

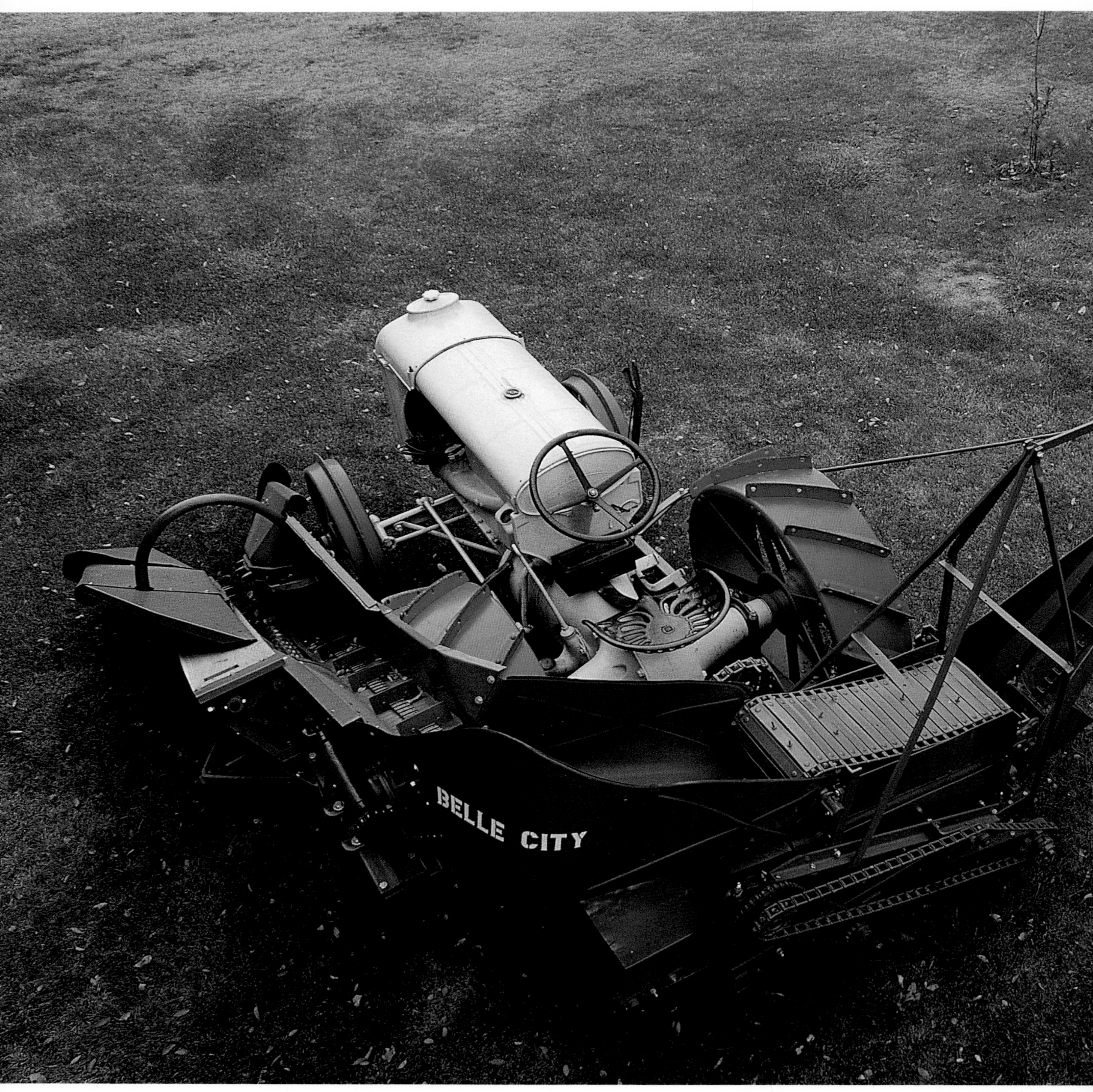

▲*This 1920 Fordson was coupled to a 1928 Belle City Corn Picker-Husker. Belle City Manufacturing was based in Racine, Wisconsin, and this example was sold through Port Huron Machine and Supply of Lincoln, Nebraska. With the spout, the entire machine stood 97in tall, 190in wide, and 160in in overall length from front to rear.*

four cylinders. Just after the new year began in 1863, Nicolaus August Otto's first four-cycle, four-cylinder, internal-combustion engine woke the neighbors. It was not perfect. It ran unsteadily. It quickly wore out seals and bearings. The engine fired strongly at first, but the cycles afterward were rough and uneven. It was months later that he recalled James Watt's application of von Guericke's atmospheric principles. The piston of Watt's steamer was pushed back by the reintroduction of atmospheric pressure to the vacuum created by the escaping steam. For Otto this meant opening the intake valve earlier.

Another patent application. Another denial in Prussia. The atmospheric principle was nothing new in Germany, and Otto's use for it was not new enough. But in London, in Paris, and in Brussels, differences were recognized and patents were granted.

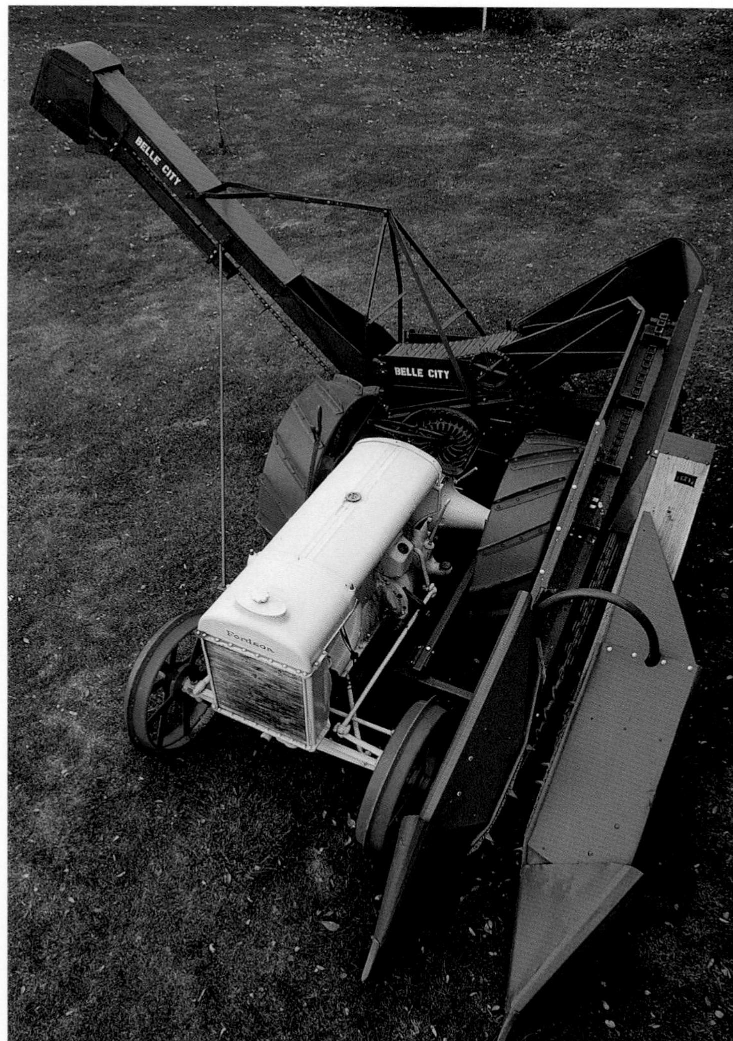

▲ *Fordson tractors were manufactured by Henry Ford in Dearborn, Michigan. Ford was unable to use his own name on the tractor because entrepreneurs in Minneapolis employed a man named Ford just to use his name on their inferior products. Henry produced his Fordson, named after Ford & Son, from 1918 through 1928.*

Now, short on money but still long on confidence, Otto found an investor, Eugen Langen, and a factory site on which to expand his experiments. N. A. Otto & Company was opened in 1864.

Work continued, and Langen, a technology institute graduate and the son of a wealthy banker, actually contributed the key to the Otto engine's success. He proposed attaching a freewheeling gear that alternately was driven by and then drove the main crankshaft. It was patented in 1866, and it was shown in May 1867 at the Paris World's Fair. In a building filled with Lenoir gas engines powering all kinds of demonstrations, Otto's new tall, single-cylinder, Greek-column-like, chattering, four-cycle gas engine consumed only one-third as much gasoline as the Lenoir. In Etienne Lenoir's hometown, Otto and Langen received the exhibition's gold medal from Napoleon III.

Success followed the gold medal, and sales followed the success: forty-six engines sold in 1868, eighty-seven in 1869, 118 in 1870. In 1871, Otto and Langen accepted 515 orders, many of them from North America.

Over the next several years, Otto continued to muse and develop. He perfected his fuel/air mixture and spark so as to burn the full length of the cylinder because the piston pulled the flaming brew to the bottom. This consumed the last unburnt fuel of the previous cycle as well. The longer stroke led to the development of Otto's high-compression engine, introduced in 1876 at his new factory in Deutz.

It would be another ten years before Gottleib Daimler and Karl Benz would incorporate Otto's engine into their first automobile. What they needed was a smaller power plant, one capable of higher speed—800, even 1000rpm, instead of Otto's few

BELLE CITY

▲*This 1920 Minneapolis 12-25 tractor strongly resembles the Waterloo Boy Model N 12-25hp tractors produced by Waterloo Gasoline Engine Co. at the same time. Minneapolis' version was to be the second-ever tractor test at the University of Nebraska, in March 1920. But it was snowed out. Retested in May, it recorded 16.3 drawbar and 26.2 belt pulley horsepower. It is owned by Walter and Bruce Keller, Kaukauna, Wisconsin.*

hundred. Otto had experimented with advancing the ignition timing as engine speed increased. Daimler licensed Otto's engine, and he financed its high-speed improvements himself.

Subjected to innumerable patent infringement suits from the mid-1870s on, Otto's engine entered the public domain in June 1890 when the Supreme Court of Justice in Germany canceled his last patent. The court knew it was too valuable to remain under control. Otto knew what that meant.

He wrote to his wife, Anna: "Now the dance will begin in earnest. Everybody and his brother will be making engines."

Within months of Otto's engine becoming available, dozens of makers throughout Europe and North America offered for sale small, single-cylinder portable, transportable, and stationary gasoline engines. These produced as little as 1hp and as much as 65hp out of single-cylinder engines and 120hp from twins. The smaller engines saw steady acceptance for use around the farms, powering everything from water pumps and corn shellers to washing machines, butter churns, and cream separators. As had been done with stationary and portable steam engines, permanent applications were set up. These were separate "power buildings" on the farm, with rooms devoted to the cleaner or the dirtier tasks, all functions powered by belts driven off of ceiling pulley shafts belted up to the engine.

At almost the same time, engineers and inventors began to adapt gasoline engines to steam traction engine frames and running gear. The development of gasoline traction engines flourished throughout North America more quickly even than Europe. In 1900, while fewer than seventy firms in North America still produced steam traction engines, more than 100 manufactured internal-combustion gasoline engines, many of these designed for use in tractors.

The Charter Gas Engine Company in Sterling, Illinois, went into business in 1882, striking up an agreement with a German immigrant engineer, Franz Burger, to produce coal oil, as

◂*Ford powered its compact, 2,700lb tractor with an in-line four-cylinder engine with 4.0x5.0in bore and stroke. Power output was rated at 9.3 drawbar and 18.2 belt pulley horsepower at 1,000rpm. The tractor and Belle City corn picker were restored and are owned by Kermit Wilke of Wilcox, Nebraska.*

▲The Minneapolis Threshing Machine Company's Model 12-25 measured 68.5in to the top of the throttle, 76in wide, and 198in long overall (about 48in longer than the similar-looking Waterloo Boy) on its 99in wheelbase (about 8in longer than the Waterloo). Front wheels were 6.0x38 while the rears were 12x56in steel with 2in tall cleats. It used automobile-type steering.

well as gasoline-fired engines, an improvement over natural gas or coal gas versions. Burger worked for the next decade producing designs that founder John Charter patented and produced. Burger's most important design, for the liquid fuel engine in September 1887, opened the way for truly portable—and transportable—power. Two years later, Charter introduced its first self-propelled gasoline traction engine made from adapting its 10 to 20hp, 160rpm engine to a Rumely steam traction engine frame and running gear.

The next year, 1890, George Taylor, a Vancouver, British Columbia, engineer, earned a patent for his worm-drive walking plow. It resembled a wheelbarrow. Its single-cylinder engine was placed above the plow moldboard. On the ground behind the plow, a screw, operated by a chain driven off the engine crankshaft, propelled the machine.

A year after that, in 1891, William Deering & Co. introduced a 6hp tricycle mower that met with some success. In 1892, John Froelich of Waterloo, Iowa, paid $1,050 for a Van Duzen No. 12 vertical single-cylinder 20hp engine that Van Duzen manufactured in Cincinnati, Ohio. Early gas engines often used open flame ignitions, but by this time, Van Duzen Gas & Gasoline Engine Co. had progressed to the hot tube-type ignition. After much effort, Froelich fit the Van Duzen to a heavily modified Robinson & Co. "Conqueror" steam traction engine chassis, and he set to work.

▲The Minneapolis used a four-cylinder vertically—and transversely—mounted engine, different from Waterloo Boy's horizontal two-cylinder. Bore and stroke measured 4.5x7.0in. The 6,600lb tractor was produced from 1920 through 1926. This example is owned by Walter and Bruce Keller of Kaukauna, Wisconsin.

Froelich worked in fields for seven weeks. He hauled his Case threshing machine behind his engine from one custom threshing job to another. He founded the Waterloo Gasoline

This was the Stockton-built version of Holt's 5-Ton model, a name which designated its gross weight, in this case, about 9,700lb. Only 212 of these machines were built in Stockton. This crawler was also referred to as the 25-45hp Caterpillar. This Caterpillar was restored by and is part of the collection of the late Joseph Heidrick, Sr., of Woodland, California.

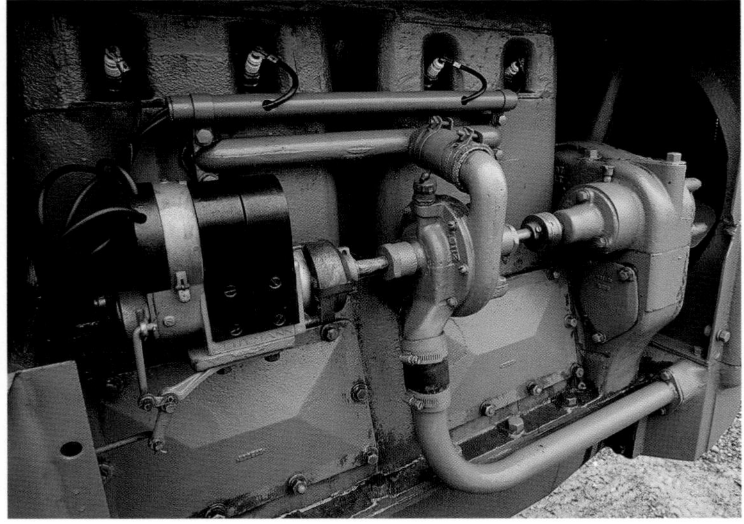

Holt's in-line four-cylinder engine has a bore of 4.75in and a stroke of 6.0in. At 1,050rpm, the engine produced just about 33hp from the drawbar. Holt fitted a Kingston carburetor and an Eisemann Model 64 magneto. The engine ran on gasoline. This M-29 was built in 1923.

Traction Engine Co. in 1893. This was an effort to capitalize on his widely publicized accomplishment; now he would build tractors for sale. But he only completed three similar machines in two years, and his partners reorganized the business.

By the end of 1892, J. I. Case Threshing Machine Co. had also tried an experimental gas tractor. Case was the first of the major steam traction engine and threshing machine manufacturers to enter the market. Designed by William Patterson, the prototype even bore his name as well as the J. I. Case logo on the canopy over the engine. Fitted on the chassis of one of Case's smaller steamers, the Patterson was a horizontal, two-cylinder, four-cycle engine.

Before the end of the century, several others made first efforts, joining the market as existing steam traction engine makers. These included the McCormick Co., Huber Manufacturing, and Kinnaird-Haines (makers of the well-known Flour City threshers).

Within the first decade of the twentieth century, the market was flooded with old names as well as new makers trying new products. Charles Hart and Charles Parr had begun experimenting with gasoline engines as college students in 1895. In 1902, they founded a manufacturing company in Charles City, Iowa, and began producing two-cylinder 15 to 30hp tractors in 1902. In 1903, fifteen were sold and Hart-Parr was established as the first manufacturing company in the United States that produced only tractors. In fact, their sales manager, W. H. Williams, claimed the first advertising use of the word "tractor" in 1906, using it to shorten the expression "gasoline traction engine." In fact, the word had appeared in a U.S. patent application, #425,600, in 1890, issued to George H. Edwards of Chicago.

In 1902, in Stockton, California, John Kroyer designed and developed his Sieve Grip tractor at his Samson Iron Works. The Samson Sieve Grip used a unique style of wide, open-tread steel wheels that combined good traction with minimal soil compaction. The tractor was built low to the ground and was introduced with a single-cylinder engine and upgraded with a smooth-running four-cylinder.

At this same time, H. M. Wallis, a son-in-law of Jerome Increase Case, was president of his own firm, the Wallis Tractor Company, located in Cleveland, Ohio. In 1902, Wallis introduced its Bear model, a ten-ton, giant tricycle tractor that remained in production for another decade. The Bear's in-line, upright, four-cylinder engine displaced 1,481ci and drove not only the two huge rear driving wheels but also a power steering system. Maneuverability was further aided with independent rear-wheel brakes. In ten years of production, reportedly, only nine Bears were manufactured despite the model's many advances over both steam engines and other gasoline tractors.

In 1912, Clarence M. Eason joined the engineering staff at Wallis, working under Robert O. Hendrickson, the chief engineer. Together, they developed the unit frame system out of boilerplate. This was the first example of using the engine to serve as part of the structure of the tractor. In 1915, their Wallis Cub appeared with its transmission enclosed in the same U-frame assembly as the engine. In 1919, with the Model K, Hendrickson extended the U-frame to the full tractor length, including the drivetrain bull gears. By that time, however, Eason had left Wallis to work for Hyatt Roller Bearing, a company that would soon supply Henry Ford with bearings and ideas about unit frame tractor construction.

In Titusville, Pennsylvania, chemical engineer A. Fasenmeyer discovered a method to remove gasoline from the natural gas that was a by-product from oil wells. Fasenmeyer compressed this gas and then slowly cooled it, passing it through pipes placed in water tanks, similar to the condenser systems used by Savery, Newcomen, and Watt. Fasenmeyer obtained the product known as "casinghead gasoline." This process, after further improvements, became known as fractioning, gasoline being one of the fractions.

Three thousand miles west, also in 1904, Benjamin Holt began experiments with gasoline engines in crawler tractors. His work producing and selling steam-powered crawlers convinced him of the continuing market for crawler tractors for the soft sandy soil of central California and for use around Sacramento, where several rivers converged to produce rich, moist, spongy loam. By 1908, his first Model 40 25hp gasoline-engine "Caterpillars" were offered for sale out of his works in Stockton, California.

At the beginning of 1906, International Harvester Co. (IHC), completed its first tractor, a single-cylinder 20hp machine using a hit-or-miss ignition and friction drive. The friction drive was replaced almost immediately with a two-speed forward/one reverse sliding gear transmission that used a friction clutch and a final drive gear. At about the same time, IHC's chief engineer Edward Johnson completed development work on twenty-five prototype 8hp, two-cylinder, air-cooled, chain-driven automobiles. These were meant to be sold to farmers through IHC's tractor and implement full-line stores. Despite IHC's early successes with trucks, the IHC car never materialized. International tractors, however, were quite successful. From then on, the company devoted its time and efforts to the areas of its expertise.

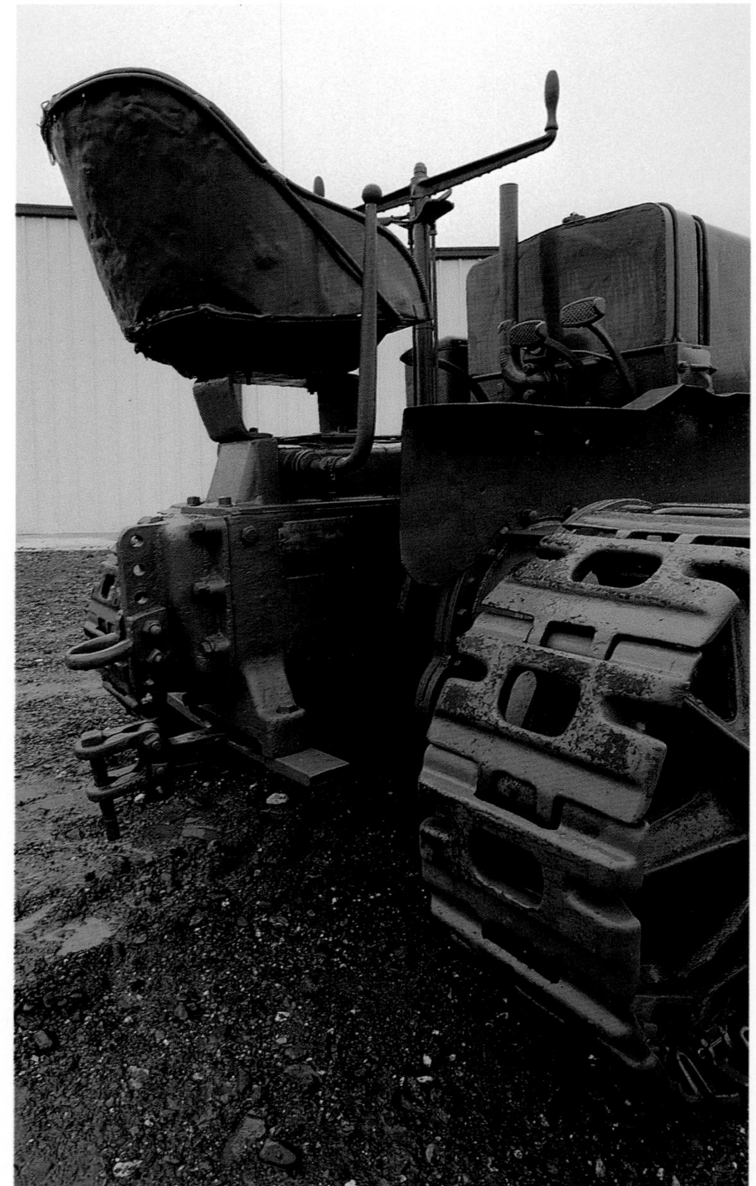

▲ *Holt used a three-speed transmission with a top speed of 5.5mph. Holt replaced this model with the 5-Ton which remained in production until Holt Manufacturing Co. in Peoria, Illinois consolidated with Best Manufacturing of San Leandro, CA and together formed the company known as Caterpillar Company in September 1925.*

In 1906, car-maker Henry Ford entered the tractor market with a 24hp, four-cylinder machine based on his Model K automobile. While it was not a perfect machine, it convinced him that if anyone could build a perfect tractor, it would be Henry Ford. Out of that conviction developed a four-decade-long competitive battle that humbled and destroyed countless manufacturers and substantially strengthened and improved every surviving tractor maker and its products.

Beginning in 1908, in an attempt to bring more information to the farmers, the Winnipeg Industrial Exhibition began to include a "Light Agricultural Motor Competition." This served not only to show farmers the capabilities of various makers, it also put the makers at risk. If their tractors were unreliable or not strong enough, they would break before an audience. Eight tractors were entered in 1908. One withdrew before the competition began, and a four-cylinder 20hp Universal broke during testing. But three tractors by International Harvester and a single entry each from Transit Thresher Co., Marshall Sons & Co., Ltd., and

▲*Both Ben Holt and Dan Best first built crawler tractors with tiller wheels mounted far out front for balance and steering. Holt's individual track clutches and brakes accomplished most of the steering; engineers in the Stockton shops relocated an engine closer to the rear and found it balanced well without the tiller. Over the years, each manufacturer produced models comparable to the other and both devoted considerable resources to legal battles over patent infringement. This 1917 Holt 75 belongs to Don Hunter, Pomona, of California*

Kinnaird-Haines Co. went through the workout. The Kinnaird-Haines four-cylinder 30hp machine won on points. The competitions continued through the July 1912 exhibition. Entered into the competition were a Sawyer-Massey four-cylinder 22 to 45hp tractor and Canadian licensees from Heer Engine Company, with its four-wheel-drive tractors, and Canadian Holt Tractor Co., with its Model 40 Caterpillar, along with twenty-five other machines.

According to the U.S. Department of Agriculture, in 1910 53.7 percent of the U.S. population, some 49,348,883 individuals, lived in rural areas. Of those, a third were engaged in agricultural occupations. In Canada, 39.9 percent of the working population, 716,937 people, worked in agriculture. Of the more than 1.9 billion acres of total area in the United States, 47,097,000 were producing wheat alone, averaging 14.7 bushels per acre. In Canada, with 2.4 billion acres of total land, barely 9,945,000 acres were producing wheat, averaging a yield of 19.7 bushels per acre.

Most gasoline tractors sold in 1910 were four-stroke engines with hit-and-miss ignition governors to control their speed. A low voltage DC magneto, or in some cases a generator, powered the ignition while the engine was running. Models equipped with electric start used dry cell batteries.

The initial ignition efforts by gas engine inventors had used an open flame that was exposed to the combustion chamber by a slide valve. This moved at the proper instant to ignite the fuel mixture on top of the piston. It worked fine for engines with little or no fuel compression, but as engineers learned that more power was produced if the fuel mixture was compressed and then ignited, a hot tube system developed. In this technique, a tube containing platinum, nickel, or even porcelain was kept hot by a flame burning inside it. The tip of the tube projected slightly into the combustion chamber. But both of these systems worked only for constant speed engines, in mostly stationary applications. When engines began to move, or when various loads required different speeds, low-voltage magneto-type systems and

high-tension coil, distributor, and spark plug systems evolved.

In the high-tension system, electric energy was increased so high that the current jumped between the electrodes of the spark plug, igniting the air and fuel mixture in the cylinder. In the lower-tension system, the spark was made inside the cylinder by bringing two electrodes together. Upon separation, the two electrodes sparked, igniting the mix. The current was produced either by chemical action that occurred in a dry cell battery or by electromagnetic action created by a dynamo, or magneto, and an induction coil.

In 1910, some 4,000 tractors, both gasoline and steam, were sold throughout North America. By 1920, 203,207 gasoline (or kerosene) tractors were manufactured, of which 29,163 were destined for export. By the end of 1910, the manufacturers had developed engines that would run on cheaper kerosene, as well as on gasoline. The Canadian Heer Engine Co.'s 25hp opposed two-cylinder produced 17.5hp in the Winnipeg tests. A Rumely Oil-Pull produced 29.5hp in the same tests. Both ran on kerosene.

The sales competition between steam traction engine and gas tractor makers was fierce, but in organized events like the Ca-

▴*The first fifty of the Model D tractors were fitted with a flimsy "ladder" style front axle. This was assembled from a variety of pieces welded together for what was presumed to be greater strength. After the fiftieth Model D, Deere & Co. went to a stronger solid two-piece casting that was welded together.*

◂*Deere's horizontal two-cylinder engine measured 6.5x7.0in bore and stroke. In University of Nebraska tests, the Model D produced 22.5 maximum drawbar horsepower at 800rpm, with a peak of 30.4hp available on the belt. Earliest Model D's used the 26in diameter spoked flywheel.*

nadian Industrial Exhibitions, the steam traction engine makers got clear glimpses of the future. In the 1912 competition, of twenty-eight tractors entered, only four were steamers and even the best of these, a J.I. Case 36hp model, was outperformed by a Rumely Type E two-cylinder and by an Aultman-Taylor 30-60.

In his 1917 book, *The Modern Gas Tractor: Its Construction, Operation, Application and Repair*, Victor Pagé's final chapter profiled the tractor designs for that year. In his opening paragraph, he summarized what the farmer could expect. "The most prominent feature noted in late tractor designs is the endeavor of builders to have light and strong tractors better adapted to general work on small- and medium-sized farms than the earlier heavy designs. The trend is unmistakably toward the small- and medium-weight machine, just as the trend in automobile designing is toward the medium-weight cars of moderate price. Tractor prices have been reduced and their use is increasing in all sections of the country."

The first gasoline tractors evolved from large, horizontal, single-cylinder, stationary engines. These were mounted on a supporting frame or chassis nearly identical to those used on steam tractors. By 1920, multiple-cylinder engines were used because they vibrated much less. The general arrangement of engine, chassis, and running gear was altered as a result. The steam tractors operated with their drive gears—and the engine parts—exposed to dust and the weather. Heavy, unfinished cast iron was used. By 1920, cut alloy steel gears ran in oil and operated somewhat like the gear-change systems on automobiles. Pressed steel in channels or I-beams had replaced the huge, heavy cast iron frames used on steamers and the early gas engine tractors. Cooling and lubrication, at first almost ignored, were largely—though not universally—accomplished by closed, pressurized systems.

It was in the preface to his book that Pagé hinted at the future: "It is not the writer's intention to underestimate the advan-

▲*Tractor company equipment changes have evolved into the kinds of minutiae that confirm history for collectors. The four slots in each spoke of the steering wheel were only used in the 1923 model year. Three appeared in 1924, two were cut into the spokes in 1925 and in 1926, Deere jumped sequence and used solid bars. This is the 1923 version.*

▸*This was the 32nd Model D tractor John Deere manufactured. Its engine was adapted from Waterloo Boy gasoline tractors which Deere & Co. purchased in 1918. However, while some of the Waterloo Boys ran on gasoline, Deere's Model Ds ran on kerosene. This rare example is owned by Lester Layher of Wood River, Nebraska.*

tages and utility of the steam tractor; it has and still is performing work of great value. The gas tractor, however, in its modern forms, is able to accomplish everything the steam propelled type can do, and has important advantages the other construction does not possess. It does not require the services of a skilled engineer to operate, it has a wider range of action, is more independent of fuel and water supply in that it does not consume much liquid in cooling, and is more economical of fuel because it utilizes a larger proportion of the potential energy or heat units of the combustible by burning it directly in the cylinders."

As Pagé pointed out, many of the large gasoline tractors were smaller than some of the smaller steamers. That weight differential translated to benefits in two ways: First, it simply made the tractors more useful to smaller acreage farmers, and second, it made them less expensive to purchase and to own than the big steamers. With the development of even cheaper fuels—kerosene, diesel fuel, and the liquefied petroleum gases already on the horizon—the handwriting was beginning to show on the walls around the steam traction engine manufacturers.

JOHN DEERE
JOHN DEERE

329 CAL 26 262

▲*The Fond du Lac kit required that the owner replace the rear wheels and tires with nine-tooth pinions. These engaged a ring gear mounted on the inside of the larger replacement steel wheels. A subframe was clamped on to the Ford frame and this extended the wheelbase nearly 2ft. The manufacturer claimed the conversion could be accomplished in 15-20min.*

◄*Don and Patty Dougherty of Colfax, California, restored and own this soft-top pickup tractor conversion manufactured by the Fond du Lac Tractor Co. of Fond du Lac, Wisconsin. Kits to convert the very popular Ford Model Ts were sold by a number of makers in the late teens and twenties for between $100 and $200. Thousands were sold but most were scrapped during iron and steel collection drives during World War II.*

▲*"The power and reliability of the Ford engine,"* Victor Pagé, *a highly regarded automobile authority, wrote in his 1918 edition of* The Model T Ford Car and Ford Farm Tractor, *"makes it possible to use this light chassis for much heavier work than one would imagine it capable of. A variety of tractor attachments are provided by which the Ford chassis may be used for light agricultural work that would ordinarily be done by several horses, such as plowing, harrowing, cultivating, etc." But, he added, "A machine which is built up of a standard touring car and a tractor attachment cannot be expected to do the same kind of work that a specially designed tractor can do." He went on in later pages to introduce the Fordson tractor.*

▲*The Ford Model T engine was designed as a unit-type power plant. The engine, flywheel, and transmission are all within the same two-piece housing. This allowed Ford to ensure perfect alignment between the crankcase and the transmission shaft. Bore and stroke of the four-cylinder engine was 3.75x4.0. Power output was quoted at about 20hp.*

▸*In the thirties, Model Ts were so cheap—at $10 to $50 each—that routine maintenance was performed only on the conversion kits; the Ts were run until they broke and then were replaced. The Fond du Lac was in competition with such companies as Convertible Tractor Corp., Curtis Form-A-Tractor Co., Handy Hank Tractor Attachment Co., Smith Form-A-Truck Co., and Uni-Ford Tractor Co., among others. More than fifty companies existed in 1920. This is a 1926 Model.*

▸*This 1929 10-20 TracTracTor was produced from 1929 through 1931. A total of 1,505 crawled out of the Chicago factory. No carrier idler wheel was used (a carrier idler wheel is a roller that holds up the track along the top of its travel between the sprocketed drive wheel at rear and the front idler). Three track rollers along the bottom kept the track in contact with the ground over any contour.*

McCORMICK-DEERING

▲*McCormick-Deering offered the Model 10-20 in both wheeled tractor versions as well as crawlers. These were called the TracTracTors. This line was introduced in 1929 with this model. A prominent engineering and visual feature was its pair of track clutches under twin cones just behind the engine panel.*

▼*The 10-20 TracTracTor used the same engine as the wheel-type Model 10-20. A vertical, in-line four-cylinder 4.25x5.0in engine produced 15.5 drawbar and 24.8 belt pulley horsepower at 1,025rpm. By this time, International produced its own magnetos while still buying carburetors from Ensign. This crawler is owned by Mrs. Edith Heidrick, widow of the late Joseph Heidrick, Sr., of Woodland, California.*

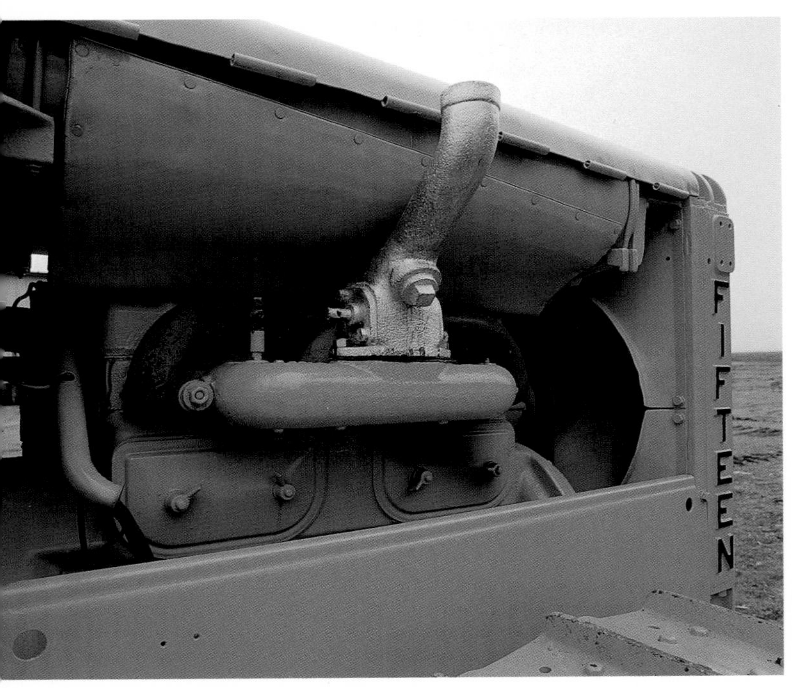

◂Bore and stroke of the in-line four cylinder engine was 3.375x4.0in. In its tests at the University of Nebraska, the Cat Model 15 produced a maximum 16.2 drawbar horsepower and 20.4hp brake horsepower at 1,500rpm. Ignition was by an Eisemann Model GV4 magneto and Caterpillar fitted Ensign carburetors on the Fifteens.

▾The tall lever is the master clutch while the two matching shorter ones operate left and right track brakes for steering. Ahead is the gear shift. Caterpillar used a three-speed transmission on the Model 15, with a top speed of 3.5mph. The 4,750lb tractor was capable of pulling a maximum of 3,105lb in first gear in its tests at University of Nebraska.

▸▸Introduced in 1929 and offered through 1932, the Model 15 sold for $1,450 at the factory in Peoria, Illinois. It used Caterpillar's own four-cylinder engine. This1929 example was restored and is owned by Frank Bettencourt of Vernalis, California. Behind the crawler is Bettencourt's John Deere-Killifer Model 7MKO-02 disk.

CATERPILLAR
FIFTEEN

◂*The 1935 Model B measured 76in tall, 79in wide, and 119in in length on an 81in wheelbase between its front and rear steel wheels. Deere used a Fairbanks-Morse DRV-2B magneto and a Schebler DLTX10 carburetor. The Model B weighed 3,275lb.*

▴*Deere's Model B engine continued on the Waterloo heritage of two-cylinder horizontal engines fitted with valves-in-head. Bore and stroke were 4.25x5.25in. Drawbar horsepower tested out at 11.8 while belt pulley output was 15.1hp at 1,150rpm. Four speeds allowed for a maximum of 6.4mph yet it was capable of pulling 1,728lb in first.*

▸▸*This was the very first Model B that was produced, number B1000. Introduced in late 1934, it was designed as a smaller, companion model to the big Model A (introduced in April 1934). It was intended to fill the shoes of two horses on any farm. This one was restored and is now owned by Walter and Bruce Keller of Kaukauna, Wisconsin.*

JOHN DEERE
GENERAL PURPOSE

Chapter Three

The Nebraska Tractor Tests

A Bogus Ford Brings Accountability To the Tractor

W. Baer Ewing had an idea for a tractor, but he needed help. He didn't need a designer or an engineer. He needed a name, and he knew the name he wanted. When he found him, Ewing hired a young man named Paul B. Ford.

Ewing was a Minneapolis entrepreneur. Involved with the Federal Securities Company in Minneapolis, he had sold bonds and securities in the Power Distribution Company. Electric power was being introduced throughout major cities, offered to businesses and home owners alike. Rural electrification was decades away, but it was anxiously awaited in the urban areas. Investors were needed to fund development and installation, but when those bonds came due, Ewing came up short and many of his investors lost out.

Somehow, Ewing emerged unscathed. He recognized a new need in the marketplace and a new opportunity for investors. Presumably he was aware from newspaper accounts that automaker Henry Ford was interested in the farm tractor. Ewing sought to capitalize on Ford's name and the success of his automobiles. With his new assistant, Paul Ford (no relation to Henry Ford), Ewing founded the Ford Tractor Co., incorporated in South Dakota probably sometime during 1915. According to C. H. Wendel in his *Encyclopedia of the American Farm Tractor* and other sources, Paul Ford knew nothing of farm tractors, but that didn't matter to Ewing who began promoting him as the designer of Ewing's new tractor, a machine actually designed by a character named Kinkaid.

To finance the tractor's production, Ewing sold stock through his own company, Federal Securities. Then he sold tractors to unsuspecting farmers. The company went broke in 1916, but Ewing managed to hold onto both the patents and designs, and to Paul Ford and his name. Ewing relocated the whole operation to southeast Minneapolis and opened his doors a second time to an unsuspecting marketplace.

▲The Fordson pulls a Ferguson-Sherman two-bottom plow attached to its Ferguson Duplex hitch. When car and tractor-maker Henry Ford would not give Irish engineer Harry Ferguson the respect he felt he deserved, Ferguson went into business with two brothers in Detroit to produce his plows and hitches. These were meant for use on—and often sold with—Fordson tractors.

▸Palmer Fossum's 1926 Fordson sits ready for the next morning's work. A homemade tin-and-wood cab was simply bolted onto the fenders. The racket it made in vibration was louder than the Ford four-cylinder 4.0x5.0in engine. At 1,000rpm, the Fordson produced 12.3 drawbar horsepower, adequate to pull a two-bottom plow across Fossum's Northfield, Minnesota, field.

His Ford Model B tractor (there was no Model A) sold for $350 and was rated at eight drawbar and sixteen belt pulley hp. He advertised that it was capable of pulling two 14in plows. It used an opposed two-cylinder Type M engine manufactured by the Gile Boat & Engine Co., of Ludington, Michigan. The few tractors produced were probably assembled just to show potential investors an actual product, to convince them of the company's viability.

Those who bought stock to capitalize the company never saw any return; those who bought one of the few machines that Ewing sold learned even more quickly of their mistake. In mid-1917, Ford Tractor Company was brought before a U.S. grand jury in New York as part of an investigation of Ewing's partner's involvement in other stock sales schemes. The partner was convicted and sentenced for conspiracy to defraud investors and, according to Wendel, Ewing relocated to Canada to organize yet another tractor company.

This kind of skullduggery was not uncommon in the first twenty years of gasoline tractor manufacturing. There were many other tractor makers organized solely for the purpose of making money, not tractors. One prototype would be produced, funds would be raised, and overnight the company was out of business, offices vacated, doors locked. The lone prototype had sold for cash to some unsuspecting victim.

One such victim, however, was in a position to do something about his misfortune. It didn't get him his money back, but almost single-handedly he cleaned up the tractor manufacturing business.

Wilmot Crozier, a progressive farmer

Fordson

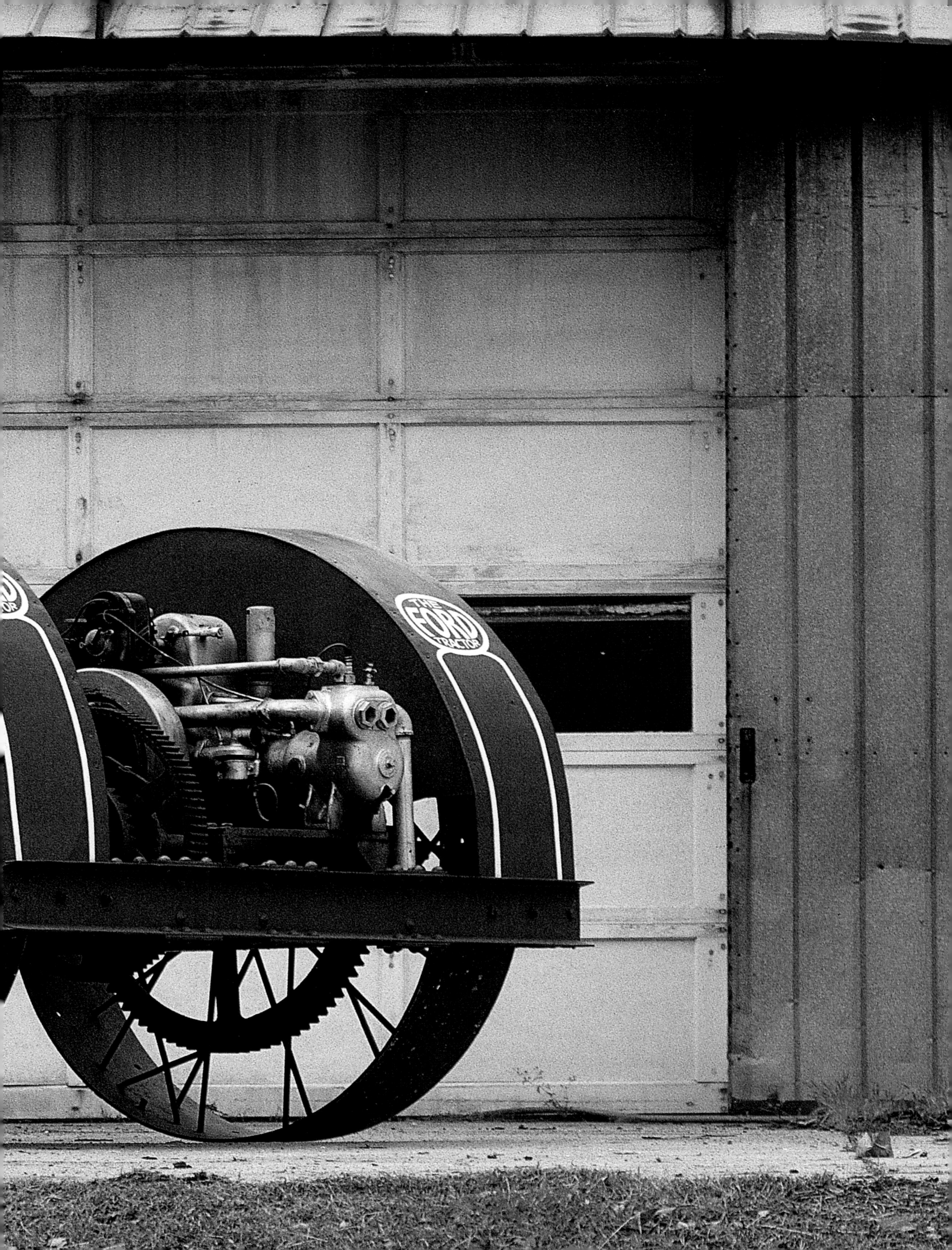
THE
FORD
TRACTOR

The Gile-engined Ford1919 Model B sold for $350 fully equipped out of its factory at 2619-2627 University Avenue S.E., in Minneapolis. Described as a two-plow tractor, it used bull gears to provide power to each of the two large front drive wheels. It incorporated automobile-type steering. Ironically, Gile Tractor and Engine Company produced its own rather innovative tractors from 1913 until late 1918.

The engine Baer Ewing selected for his Ford tractor was manufactured by Gile Boat and Engine Company of Ludington, Michigan. It was the Type M, rated to operate between 700 and 900rpm, and quoted as producing eight drawbar and sixteen belt horsepower. There's no way to prove it because, of course, its very unreliability brought about the Nebraska tractor tests.

from eastern Nebraska, bought one of Baer Ewing's Ford Model B tractors in 1916. The machine broke down so frequently that he demanded a replacement and got from Ewing a 1917 model. It was no better so he simply gave up and parked it. He replaced it with a 1917 Bull tractor, and it too failed him. Soon after, in 1918, still desiring tractor power for his farm, Crozier bought a second-hand Rumely Oil-Pull that worked better than his expectations. Rated at three-plows, the Rumely routinely handled five with no difficulty through the soil on his farm.

Crozier, college educated and world traveled—he had served four years as a superintendent of schools in the Philippines—was angered by his experience and frustrated by his mechanical innocence. He had read a farm journal editorial that recounted experiences similar to his own. The article called on the farm tractor manufacturing industry to clean its own house or face government regulation.

Newspapers in rural areas and farm journals at this time were strong advocates for farmers' rights and needs. Strong editorial support led manufacturers to produce smaller, more maneuverable tractors early on; these same printed voices encouraged the creation and development of general purpose tractors capable of more functions than merely initial field plowing, preparation, and planting. The role of these publications in the development of farm tractors was significant.

According to R. B. Gray in his 1975 book, *The Agricultural Tractor: 1855-1950*, as early as 1915 there was a growing interest in a federal government-established national testing station for farm equipment. Whether the Bureau of Standards would operate it or the Department of Agriculture was one of many ques-

The Model B measured 60in high, 78in wide, and 124in long overall. Its front wheels—the driving wheels—were 54in in diameter. Steering was by the rear wheel only; there were no separate clutches or brakes for either front wheel. The drawbar could swivel as much as fifteen degrees to either side of center.

J-61

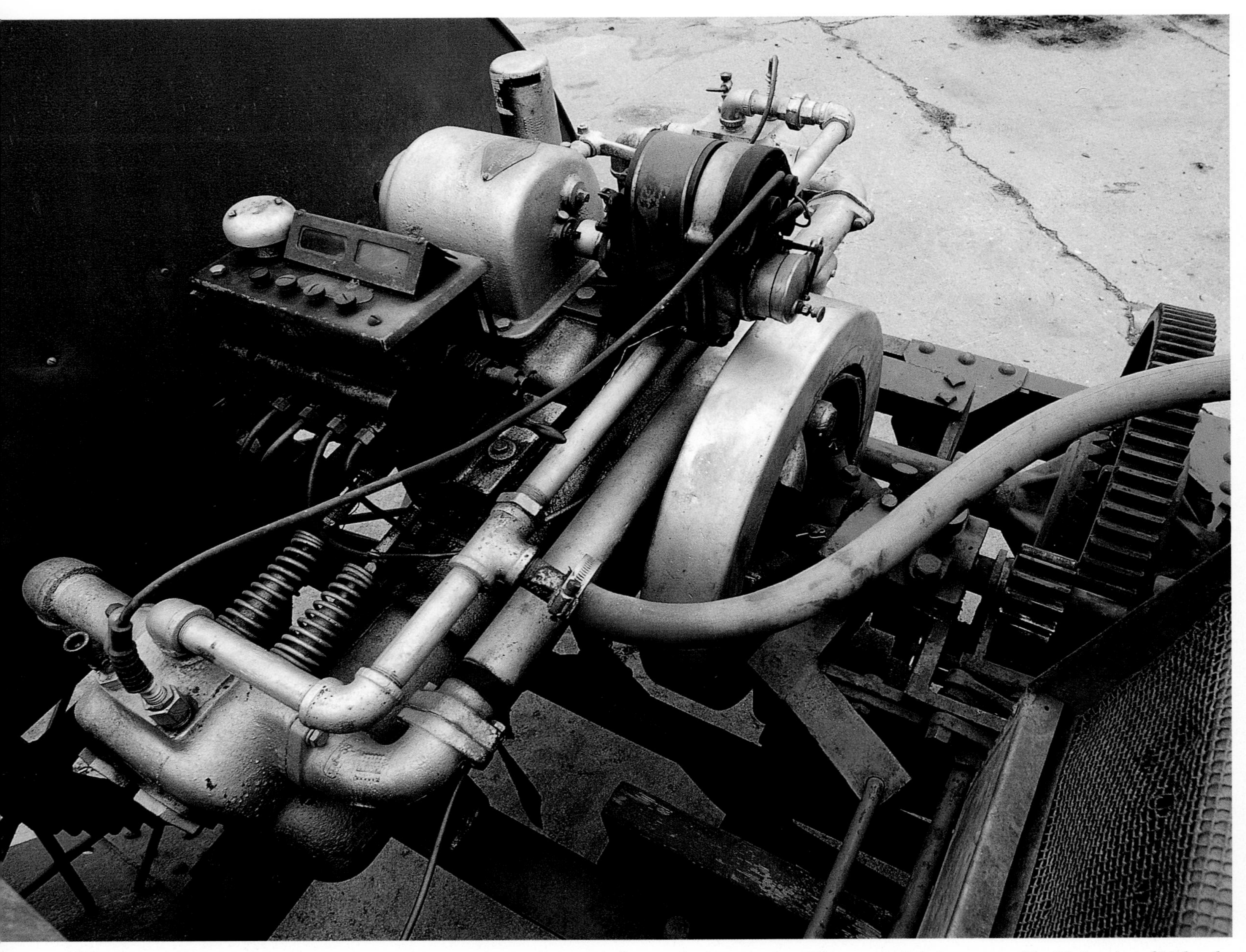

▲*The front wheels were 54in in diameter. The entire tractor measured 60in tall, 78in wide, and 124in overall length. A Bennett Model EB carburetor and International Harvester's Model E4A magneto were standard equipment. This tractor is being restored by University of Nebraska agricultural engineering students Jeff Hays and Brent Smith.*

tions to be answered. The American Society of Agricultural Engineers advocated formation of a Bureau of Agricultural Engineering within the Department of Agriculture. All that was needed was funding.

Crozier, elected to a two-year term to the Nebraska State Legislature in 1919, approached several of his fellow legislators with the idea of a testing system, carried out by impartial judges. This would evaluate any tractor that was offered for sale in the state of Nebraska. The results would be public knowledge; if the tractor failed—or passed—everyone could know it. Surely a manufacturer that knew its tractors would not succeed the tests would not offer them, and therefore, no farmer in Nebraska would have to go through Crozier's experience again.

The Department of Agricultural Engineering at the University of Nebraska was chosen as the suitable testing facility, and on July 5, 1919, it was law. No new tractor could be sold legally in Nebraska without a permit, issued by the State Railway Commission. The permit, certified by a board of engineers, would

▲*As significant as Henry Ford's Fordson was in farm tractor history, this Ford tractor built by a Minneapolis manufacturer to take advantage of the Ford name started a revolution in tractor manufacturing. W. Baer Ewing named the machines after an employee, Paul B. Ford, and produced them in Minneapolis. Nebraska tractor tests began due to the poor performance of these tractors. Ironically, this one is owned by the University of Nebraska Tractor Testing Museum. The museum is operated by its founder and former test director, Lester Larsen.*

prove the tractor had substantiated the claims of its manufacturer by a series of standard tests and procedures.

L. W. Chase, head of the department at the Lincoln campus, had also been actively involved in the Winnipeg Agricultural Motor Contests. He hired Claude K. Shedd from Ames, Iowa, to be engineer-in-charge of testing. Through the winter, the necessary procedures were devised and set up. Little money was available, and a small building was quickly erected, and equipment put in place. On March 31, 1920, the tests began. Ten days later, a Waterloo Boy Model N 12-25 passed the first Nebraska tractor test.

Tractor makers with nothing to fear applauded the tests nearly as loudly as did Nebraska farmers. Tractor makers like Baer Ewing wisely stayed out of Nebraska. The eighteenth test performed at the university facility was Henry Ford's own tractor, called the Fordson because, through Ewing's shrewdness, Henry Ford did not own the rights to his own name for farm tractor manufacture. He called his Detroit company Ford & Sons.

▸▸*Early Waterloo Boy tractors used the slack-chain steering mechanism. This allowed the front axle to pivot back and forth against the coil springs at the ends to cushion shock to the operator's hands on the steering wheel. It also required some advance thinking to take up the slack before a tight turn.*

WATERLOO BOY

GASOLINE ENGINE CO. WATERLOO, IOWA
Waterloo Boy
KEROSENE TRACTORS

◂*Tested at Nebraska University's main campus in Lincoln, the Model N used Waterloo Gasoline Engine Company's horizontal two-cylinder engine with 6.5x7.0in bore and stroke. This engine style set a precedent with Deere & Co. that would continue from the time Deere bought Waterloo in March, 1918 until engines changed in 1960.*

▴*The Waterloo engine produced 15.9 drawbar horsepower and 25.9hp on the belt pulley. The Model N was introduced in 1917 and remained in production until 1924 when Deere and Company brought out its Model D. A two-speed transmission enabled the Waterloo to pull 2,900lb at 750rpm in first gear. This 1920 example is owned by Walter and Bruce Keller of Kaukauna, Wisconsin.*

▸▸*Once Nebraska Legislator/educator Wilmot Crozier succeeded in getting tractor tests mandated by state law, the legitimate companies lined up with their products, anxious for approval. The first tractor tested was a Waterloo Boy Model N similar to the one shown here. It passed the tests.*

KEROSENE
WATERLOO BOY

▲ *Allis-Chalmers specified the Kingston Model L carburetor and an Eisemann GS4 magneto. Tested at the University of Nebraska, the Allis four-cylinder 4.75x6.5in engine produced 33.2 drawbar and 44.3 belt pulley horsepower at 930rpm.*

▸ *Original and unrestored, Conrad Schoessler's 1929 Model E needs only its seat to be complete. Introduced in 1919 as the Model 18-30, it was improved and uprated to 20-35 by 1929. It remained in production through 1930. About 2,155 were sold.*

▸▸ *The Model E weighed 7,095lb for testing yet pulled 4,400lb in the lower of its two gears. While the tractor was introduced at a selling price of more than $2,000, the fierce competition generated by price wars between Henry Ford and International Harvester reduced the price of all machines. By late 1928, the Model E 20-35 was selling for $1,295.*

Chapter Four

Development of the Diesel

The Power and the Glory

The engine's German inventor had it in mind to call it the Delta engine, or possibly, "The Excelsior." On paper, he referred to it as the "Rational Heat Engine on the Diesel Patent," but while he was agonizing over its name and fretting so many other problems in early October 1895, his wife, Martha, said to him, "Just call it a Diesel engine."

Rudolf Diesel, a German born in Paris in 1858, had an idea for the engine while he was still a teenager. His higher education included several years at the School of Industry in London when his family lived there. He had earned a degree in engineering from Munich's Polytechnikum before he was twenty. Exposed to the theories and engines of Thomas Newcomen, James Watt, and Nicolaus Otto, Diesel challenged himself to invent a heat engine that was more powerful and more efficient than anything achieved by those three men whom he admired most.

Out of school in 1880, Diesel's first job was in a plant owned by Carl Linde, his former professor of theoretical mechanical engineering in Munich. Linde had invented a machine to make artificial ice using pressurized ammonia.

Working for Linde furthered Diesel's practical education. Gaseous ammonia can be condensed into liquid at about 50deg Fahrenheit under six to seven atmospheres—nearly 100psi—of pressure. Boiling it back to a gas consumes a great deal of heat out of, for example, a water reservoir. Simply put, returning liquid ammonia to gas will chill water to ice, condensing water to its extreme. This, of course, is exactly the opposite effect of a heat engine.

Diesel imagined that an engine might be made to work by compressing ammonia under perhaps fifty atmospheres. This could be done by cooling it—compressing it—rapidly through the action of a piston in a cylinder. When the ammonia was reheated, the increased pressure would force that piston back. But liquid ammonia is a corrosive, and when his pipes leaked, the air around his "engine" became lethal. After five years of experiments (Diesel was nothing if not tenacious and thorough), he gave up on ammonia. By 1890, he had revised his idea and he began to conceive of a high-pressure air engine, the air heated quite hot by extreme compression. Into a cylinder filled with highly compressed air, a fine mist of fuel would be injected when the air was at its most compressed stage. An explosion should result, and this explosion would force the piston back down the cylinder. His paper on this theory, published in 1893, earned him his first patent.

▲*The Farmall M was introduced in August 1939 and became one of International's most successful and largest-selling tractors by the time it was discontinued in 1952 when it was replaced by the Super M series. In all, 279,821 of the Model M were produced. The electric starter and lights were optional in 1940, as was the power take-off and belt pulley.*

▸*The Farmall diesel Model M was announced in 1940 with production beginning in 1941 and continuing through 1954. It sold for $1,550. It was available in standard and row-crop fronts and by 1947, the high-clearance V-series was offered. A total of 8,298 gasoline MV and diesel MDV tractors were sold.*

Diesel's engine operated on the basis of Nicolaus Otto's four-cycle gasoline engine. But Otto's second stroke, the compression of fuel and air mix just before spark, became Diesel's compression stroke with plain air alone. Diesel's engine achieved six to eight times more compression than Otto's engine was intended to accomplish.

This high pressure heated the air at the top of the stroke so much that all Diesel needed to do was to introduce a volatile fuel mixture; no spark was necessary. The air was hot enough to immediately ignite the mix. It confirmed Diesel's theories. The cylinder's contents would explode through the third cycle, pushing the piston down as the combustion expanded the mixture in the cylinder. Exhaust followed on the fourth stroke, just the same as Otto's engine.

It required years of experiments to make it work. If he succeeded, his engine would provide significant fuel economy over gasoline engines. Because of this possibility, he was able to convince Machienenfabrik Augsburg to give him space in which to work. Industrialist Friedrich Krupp provided the financial backing with which to

DIESEL
McCORMICK
FARMALL
MDV

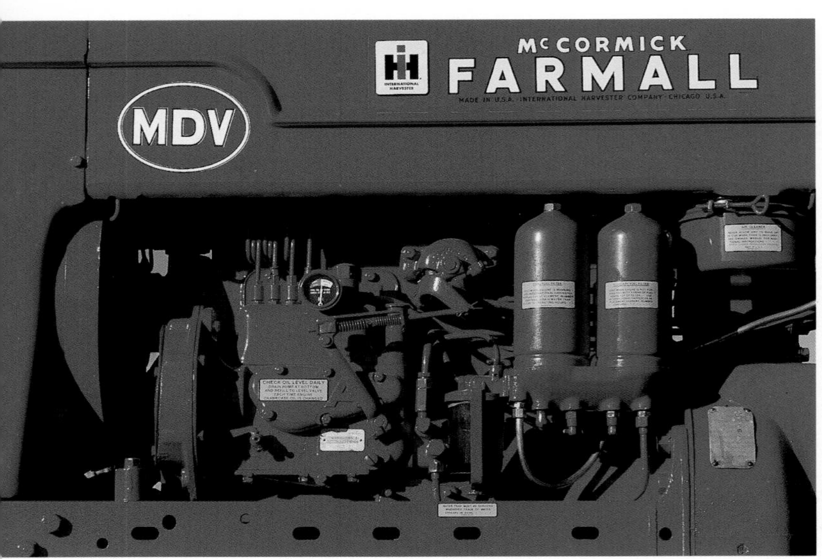

▲*International's in-line vertical four-cylinder engine measured 3.875in bore and 5.25in stroke. It used a Bosch fuel-injection system. In its 1941 University of Nebraska tests, it produced 25.4 drawbar horsepower and 35.0 horsepower on the belt pulley. In its lowest gear it was capable of pulling 4,541lb; in its highest gear, it would run more than 16mph on the road.*

▸*The high clearance V-series yielded 28in of crop headroom under the drawbar. Overall the tractor stood 113in tall, 83in wide, and 141in long overall. Front tires were 7.50-20 while rears were 12.4-38s. This 1947 MDV is owned by Bob Pollock of Denison, Iowa.*

experiment. Diesel started in July 1893. By mid-1895, his first experimental engine was ready. With a crude fuel pump injecting a petrol mixture into his cylinder, which generated eighteen atmospheres of pressure, about 250psi, his theoretical engine fired at last. One time. He had wanted thirty atmospheres, but achieving it was impossible with the technology available at the time. It was a good thing. A pressure gauge that he had fitted to the top of the cylinder exploded from his engine's internal pressure. Pieces flew like shrapnel around his lab.

But it did prove that Diesel was right. His theory worked. It simply needed more work. Much more work, that is, because his engine would not yet run continuously. However, by 1897, Diesel had developed a fuel pump that operated at a pressure that was even higher than that of the air compressed within his cylinder. His new pump would blast the fuel mix into the cylinder at just the critical instant. This fuel-feed system lasted virtually unaltered until sometime in 1923, when Robert Bosch perfected his own high-pressure injection fuel pump.

Diesel's follow-up experiments with a multi-cylinder engine were a disaster. At the same time, Adolphus Busch, the St. Louis, Missouri, brewery owner, came to Munich to see Diesel. After thoroughly examining the engine and getting the opinions of other theoretical scholars and practical engineers, Busch watched some experiments. Then he signed a contract with Diesel in October 1897. Busch would produce diesel engines in the United States. Diesel, full of himself, asked Busch for a license fee of $1 million! Busch never blinked. And in 1898,

▸▸*There's plenty of work ahead for Frank Bettencourt's D-6. Behind the crawler is his freshly restored John Deere No. 8 four-bottom 16in deep-tillage plow. This plow configuration is known as a three-by-four, the fourth plow positioned off to the left of the three main plows. Bettencourt restored both the plow and crawler for his collection at Vernalis, California.*

McCORMICK
FARMALL
MDV
DIESEL

Caterpillar Diesel
CATERPILLAR
CATERPILLAR
D6
CAT
D6

▲*The D-6 was a powerful choice for agriculture in California's central valleys. The six-cylinder engine of 4.5x5.5in bore and stroke operated at 1,450rpm and produced 49.4 drawbar and a maximum of 76.9 brake horsepower during its Nebraska tests in July 1949. The 18,805lb tractor pulled a maximum weight of 16,222lb, clearly demonstrating the efficiency of crawler tractors.*

▼*The starting engine transmits its power through a single-plate clutch to a sliding pinion which is engaged with the diesel engine flywheel gear by means of a hand lever. The pinion is automatically disengaged by centrifugal force acting on the pinion latches when the diesel engine begins to operate under its own power.*

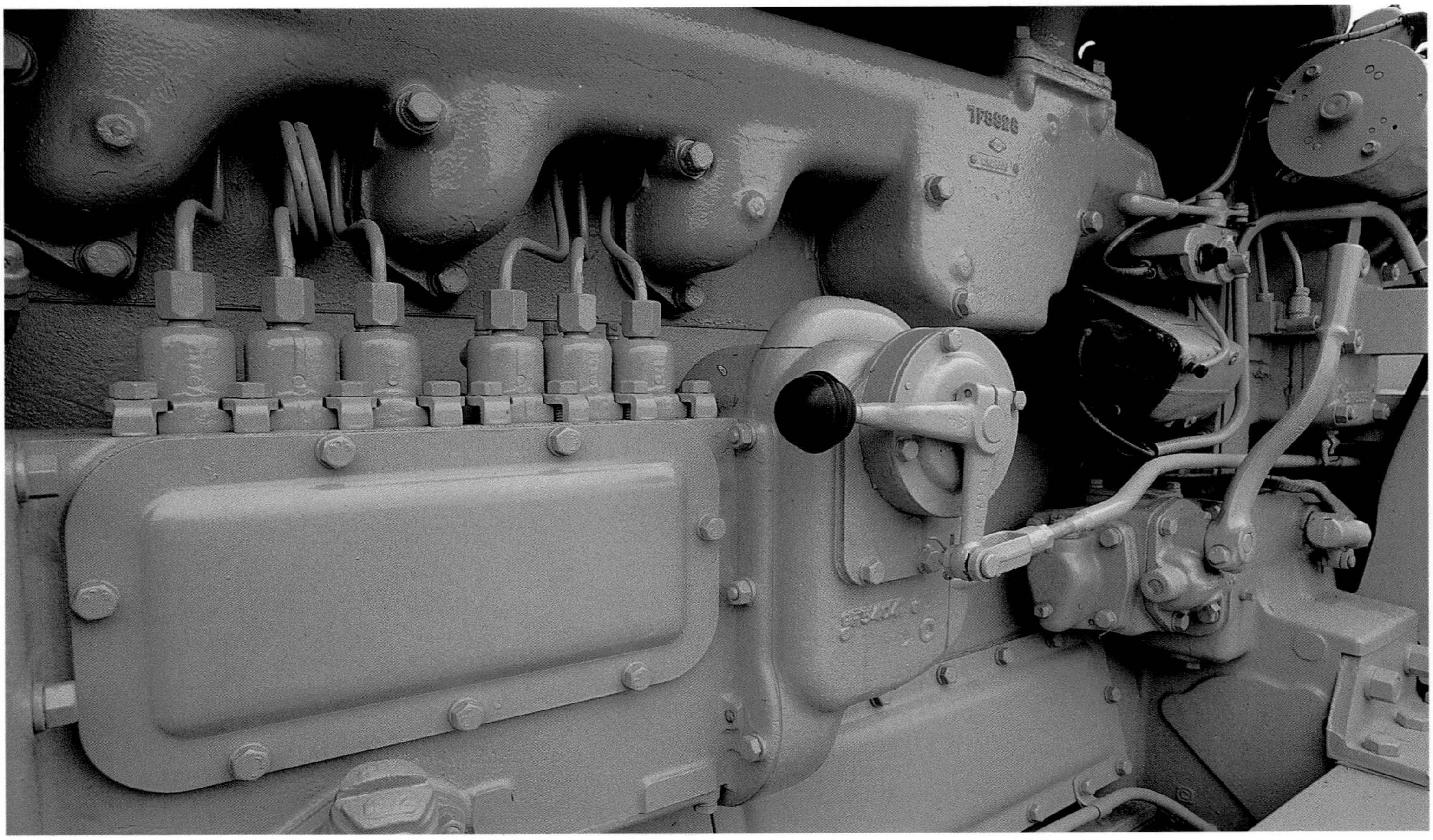

▲ *Caterpillar spent more than $1 million dollars during the late 1920s to develop and prove the diesel engine for use in mechanized agriculture. Introduced on the Caterpillar 60 chassis as the 1C-series in 1931, diesel power was not an immediate success. It was something new and as yet unproven. By the fifities, however, diesel was nearly all that Caterpillar sold. This is the 1952 Model D-6.*

Busch began manufacturing the first diesels in North America.

With his own newfound wealth to fund his work, Diesel began to develop practical uses for his engine. The French and the Russians had diesels in canal boats just after the turn of the century. Around 1904, Diesel began to imagine his engines adapted to locomotives and automobiles. By 1912, his large engines were in ships, and the Sulzer Brothers, a locomotive works in Winterthur, Switzerland, were first to experiment with a diesel to replace steam power. But those efforts failed several times. The mechanics came to call the Sulzer engine "The Foundry." With each failure, its heat melted the internal parts.

The world had come to understand what Diesel knew. His engine, when run alongside Nicolaus Otto's gasoline version, used as little as one-third the amount of fuel to produce comparable work. A group of American engineers came to Germany in early 1913 to invite Diesel to appear with his engine at the San Francisco Panama-Pacific Exhibition in 1915. He would sail to the United States on a diesel-powered ship.

But Rudolf Diesel had been psychologically troubled from the first by his failures. Then, following his indisputable success, he was plagued even more by the jealousy and treachery of competitors who tried to steal his invention or by critics who sought to revile it. And so on Monday, September 29, 1913, sailing on the North Sea from Hamburg to England to supervise the opening of his engine factory in Ipswich, Rudolf Diesel simply slipped over the side of the ship late in the night. His body was found and identification was confirmed days later. But because fishermen customarily did not take dead bodies from the sea, they let his body drift away.

It fell to Robert Bosch—maker of magneto sparking devices for airplanes, automobiles, trucks, and tractors—to substitute Diesel's high-air-pressure fuel-injection system with hydraulic injection of the mixture into the cylinders. Bosch's work commenced shortly after the November 1918 World War I armistice. A number of engineers and experimenters had begun working to develop a reliable fuel feed system for diesel engines. By late 1922, Bosch was seriously involved, and for the next four years, he and his engineers attempted to devise methods of blasting a microscopic drop of fuel as many as twenty times a second into a diesel combustion chamber against high back pressure.

By 1927, trucks from Benz, Daimler, and MAN (Machienenfabrik Augsburg had evolved into MAN around the time of Diesel's death) took to the road in a driving test that went from southern Germany through Czechoslovakia, Austria, France, and back into Germany. Bosch's pump on Diesel's engine was reliable enough that three more Benz diesel trucks be-

ALLIS-CHALMERS
WD
45

▲*Standard equipment on the WD-45 included the automatic traction booster, two-clutch power control, a five-way hydraulic system, a four-speed transmission, power take-off, individual foot-operated rear wheel brakes, an adjustable hydraulic shock-absorber seat, fenders, twelve-volt electric starter, and lights.*

◂*Allis-Chalmers introduced the WD tractor line in 1948 with a four-cylinder 226ci high compression gasoline engine available as a standard, adjustable wide front end, and both a dual-wheel and single-wheel row crop front ends. In 1955, Allis added its new overhead valve, six-cylinder 230ci diesel.*

gan making shuttle runs between various Bosch factories in Europe. Another one was shipped to New York in late 1927 for deliveries in the East. Bosch delivered its one thousandth diesel engine fuel-injection pump before 1928. At that point, it was ready to gear up for the mass production that it believed the world's industry would demand.

Diesel engines did make it to San Francisco for the Panama-Pacific Exposition. One, a McIntosh & Seymour four-cylinder produced 500hp at 164rpm and won grand prize at the exhibition. Another, displayed by the Danish licensee Burmeister & Wain, operated a generator in the Machinery Building, not far from where Best Tracklayer and Holt Caterpillar gasoline-engine tractors were shown. C. L. Best, son of founder Daniel Best, was running the Best company at the time, and he and his chief engineer, Oscar Starr, came frequently to the exhibition to see, study, and ask questions about the diesel engine. Its economy of operation convinced both men that it was necessary to get some version of it into a tractor.

Shortly after Adolphus Busch was licensed to produce diesel engines in St. Louis, another American visited Dr. Diesel during his early trips to Ipswich in 1911 and obtained production rights (Diesel had been granted several honorary degrees following the success of his engine). George A. Dow, a pump manufacturer

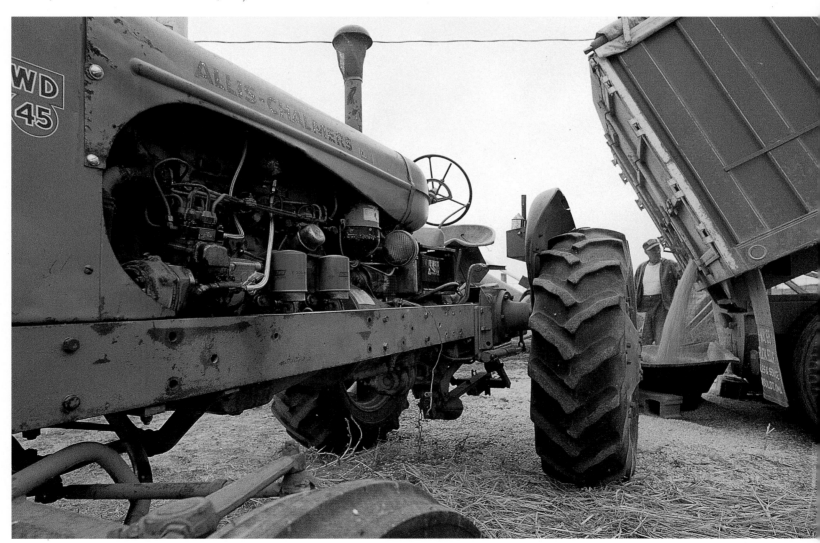

▲*The new six-cylinder engine displaced 3.45x4.125in bore and stroke. Drawbar horsepower was measured at 30.5 at 1,625rpm, and a maximum of 43.3hp was measured on the belt pulley. In addition to drawbar and belt pulley power, an additional engine use was the "Minute-Quick" system that used engine power to adjust rear wheel track.*

▸▸*The standard front axle model weighed 4,785lb and measured 88.3in tall and 128in long. Front tires were 5.50x16; rears were 12x28, mounted on 12in steel rims. This 1955 Model WD-45 diesel is owned and used nearly every day by Clyde McCullough of Vail, Iowa.*

ALLIS-CHALMERS
WD
45

No
Grease

◂*The Marshall engine was a transverse-mounted, two-stroke, single-cylinder, horizontal diesel with a bore and stroke of 6.5x9.0in. Early models rotated counterclockwise; the final series tractors reversed crankshaft rotation. Marshall rated the tractor at 40hp at 750rpm. The radiator was split with the cooling fan placed in between the two halves. The Field Marshall measured 83in tall, 75in wide, and 113in in overall length with a 61in wheelbase. This compact, unusual tractor belongs to Walter and Bruce Keller of Kaukauna, Wisconsin.*

from Alameda, California, only a few short miles from the Panama-Pacific Exhibition site, received his license from the English makers in Ipswich.

Dow built twenty-eight diesels, all of them for marine installations, except the first one he built. That one Dow installed at his shops (and it continued running in daily use until 1952, forty years after its manufacture). These were three-cylinder 150hp engines. He manufactured diesel pumps until their price became too much of an issue with his customers, and then Dow quit rather than compromise his standards.

In the years following the 1915 exposition, Best and Starr maintained close contact with Dow. In late 1925, following the consolidation of Best and Holt operations under the name Caterpillar Tractor Company, Best, as the new Caterpillar chairman, found time to see Dow again.

Dow's diesel engineer was Art Rosen, a young mechanical engineer from the University of California. Rosen was available because Dow was quitting diesel manufacture. Ironically, Art Rosen had begun writing to the Holt company as early as July 1923. He hoped to interest Holt Manufacturing into applying the diesel to its tractors.

Meanwhile, farther up the east side of the San Francisco Bay, John Lorimer began building diesels for Atlas Imperial Company of Oakland in 1920. The Atlas diesels soon found applications in drag line and scoop shovels, fishing boats, and locomotives. The Atlas diesels were what sent Henry J. Kaiser in to see C. L. Best, Oscar Starr, and the young Art Rosen. "If you won't put Atlas Diesels in your Cat chassis," he reportedly said in frustration one day, "then I will!"

Kaiser had first pressured the tractor companies to adopt the diesel in the mid-twenties. John Lorimer and his son Ralph installed Atlas diesels in Caterpillar and Monarch crawlers.

Kaiser took three of the diesel-engine hybrids to a construction site on the Mississippi River. He discovered that the stationary-type Atlas engines were meant for use in an application that was far more structurally rigid and in an atmosphere much more environmentally controlled than what existed with an earthmoving crawler tractor. The heavy engines destroyed the Monarch and stressed a Caterpillar Sixty chassis to the breaking point.

But while Kaiser's experiences 2,000mi away from Caterpillar's headquarters in Peoria, Illinois, argued for a go-slow attitude, an event 12,000mi away injected fresh fuel against the back pressure of corporate resistance.

▴*There are a variety of ways to start the Field Marshall diesel. A special holder fit into the cylinder head to hold a kind of wick which was lit by a match. The decompression valve was opened, and the huge, heavy 25x5in flywheel could be levered around by a couple of strong men. Otherwise, another holder in the cylinder head would hold a blank shotgun shell. The operator would release the compression after the wick had burned into the engine. The shotgun shell would be fired with its holder. The tractor would almost inevitably start. It is not known how many times this could be done before the lower end of the engine needed rebuilding. This 1952 model belongs to Walter and Bruce Keller.*

◂*Field Marshall tractors were manufactured at the Britannia Works of Marshall of Gainsborough in Linconshire, England, from 1949 through 1952. During those three years, more than 3,000 tractors were produced. The tractor weighed 6,500lb and was fitted with a three-speed transmission that provided a top speed of probably 7mph. Later models used a six-speed-plus-two-reverse gear box that gave a road speed of 11.3mph.*

Even in the late twenties, heavy plowing in many places in the world was still done with cable tackle systems. In areas where sugar cane, beets, and cotton were raised, two steam engines were hired, one placed on either side of the field.

But gas-engined Caterpillars had outperformed the steamers—even those with cable rigs—everywhere. J.& H. McLaren of Leeds or G. J. Fowler of St. Ives, England, the foremost promoters and practitioners of this technique, had generally conceded defeat to gas engine Caterpillar crawlers by this time. Now a cotton-plowing contest was proposed to pit a Caterpillar Sixty against a cable system. The Sixty would run lengthwise in the fields, and while it would leave head lines in the turns, it was expected to prove more efficient than the steam and cable plowing system.

So, in early 1927, Caterpillar shipped a gasoline Model Sixty and spare parts to Khartoum in the Anglo-Egyptian Sudan. Fowler did not show up with a steam tractor, but instead arrived with tractors that had Benz diesels in them. Caterpillar was beaten by a fifty-year-old system powered by a brand new engine. Peoria cabled its representative at the contest to go to Germany and buy one of the Benz engines. There were delays, but the engine finally arrived, and Caterpillar studied it.

Then Rosen and Starr designed the engine that came to be known as the D-9900, the Caterpillar diesel engine. They initially built three engines. When those prototypes were assembled and running, the whole board of directors came out to the lab. The board had learned that engineering had spent $45,000 to build the three engines. It couldn't imagine what could require so much expenditure, but it would take much more. Caterpillar spent more than $1 million on the diesel before ever marketing the first one.

In the Experimental Section of the engineering department in the late twenties and early thirties, the first diesels were installed in a Model Sixty chassis. From the beginning, methods of starting the diesel engine had to be made foolproof, like the engine itself, otherwise it would never sell. Gasoline "pony" engines were used almost from the start.

On some of the prototypes, engineers tried to start up the small gas engine with a flat belt. They ran it until it was hot and then piped the hot water through the larger diesel to warm it up. When it was hot, the valves were dropped, and the diesel was turned over for a period to heat it up evenly enough to stabilize the combustion process. Engineers learned that it was critical to quickly disconnect the belt between the gas engine and the diesel, because when that diesel started, it would tear the gas engine to pieces.

After Henry Kaiser's experience with the Atlas diesel flexing and overstressing the Caterpillar Sixty chassis, the engineering department knew it had to strengthen the frame and solve all the other engineering problems. A special large transmission was finally used for the diesel engine tractors. It was geared down more for the diesel than was normal for the old spark-ignition gas engines.

Caterpillar finally sent out the new engine into practical field use on September 14, 1931. This model, designated the 1C series,

Old Tusko

changed the sound and style of Caterpillars—and eventually of all other tractor makers—forever. The prototype, number 1C-1, stayed with Caterpillar in the San Joaquin Valley, California, for testing and development. The four-cylinder engine displaced 1,090ci. In all, 157 of the new series of Diesel Sixties were produced.

Once the problems were sorted out, the advantages—which Henry Kaiser understood earlier and better than most—became clear. In 1932, gasoline for agriculture sold for fourteen to sixteen cents per gallon; whereas, diesel fuel was available at four to seven cents a gallon. In early field tests the Diesel Sixty prototypes performed well under heavy workloads while consuming only four gallons per hour.

Caterpillar carefully monitored who purchased its early diesels. So much was at stake. Breakdowns could be costly in time lost from work, but not only to the new tractor's owner. The effect on Caterpillar's reputation could be deadly. Engineers

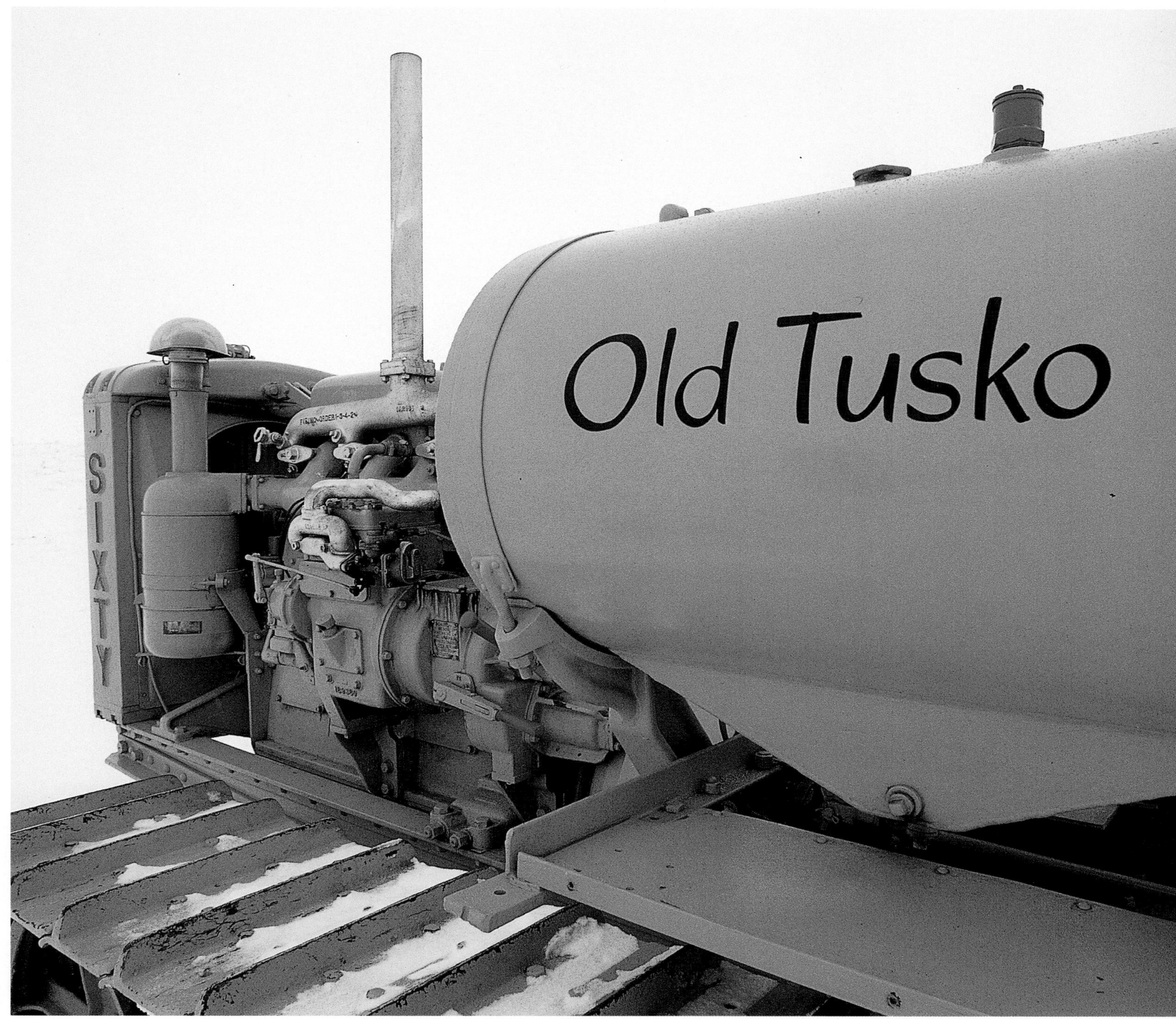

◂*This was the twelfth diesel Caterpillar sold, delivered to Mark Weatherford at Fairview Ranch in Arlington, Oregon. The first dozen diesels went to hand-picked locations where Caterpillar engineers could quickly reach them if there was a problem. The diesel was relatively easily started—even in winter storms—using its self-contained two-cylinder gasoline engine. The 25,860lb tractor could pull 11,991lb in low gear.*

▴*Original owner Mark Weatherford's children nicknamed the crawler "Old Tusko" after an elephant at the Portland Zoo. The diesel engine displaced 6.125x9.25in and it produced 54 drawbar and 77.1 brake horsepower at 700rpm. Exhaust from the small two-cylinder gasoline engine was directed toward the diesel cylinder walls and the fuel injectors. Its power was transmitted through a sliding pinion gear that engaged the diesel engine flywheel gear through the action of a hand-lever-operated clutch. Once the diesel engine began to run under its own power, centrifugal force acting on the pinion latches automatically disengaged the pinion.*

▲*Weatherford was a tractor-maker's ideal customer. He kept detailed records especially during his first year of use. Working twenty-three hours days, Old Tusko plowed 149.8 acres a day for forty-six days. His total cost was $535.81 for the entire job, averaging 7.8 cents per acre. Caterpillar diesels achieved 13.87/hp-hours per gallon of fuel in tests at University of Nebraska. In 1935 Mark Weatherford sold Old Tusko to Allen Anderson and his family nearby who recently restored the historical tractor.*

▸*Ford Motor Company, Ltd, of Dagenham, Essex, England, produced both the Major (in the background) and the Dexta. The Major was powered by Ford's in-line four-cylinder 3.94x4.52in engine that produced a maximum of 38.5 belt and 27.7 drawbar horsepower at 1,600rpm. The Major returned fuel economy of 13.93hp-hours per gallon. Both the 1958 Dexta and 1953 Major are owned by Carlton Sather of Northfield, Minnesota.*

went along with the first deliveries, staying on site for days to make certain no problems appeared. Mark Weatherford was an early purchaser of one of the diesels. He took delivery of Number 1C-12 early in March 1932 at his ranch in Oregon. For his own curiosity, he kept detailed records of his first work with the tractor. Between March 4 and April 27, 1932, Weatherford plowed 6,880 acres, averaging 149.8 acres per twenty-three-hour day. Even with the Oliver twelve-bottom 16in plow, Weatherford's diesel consumed 5,440 gallons of 7 1/2-cent-per-gallon diesel fuel. Adding in all the other costs of lubricating and transmission oils and one $2.99 repair, it cost him $535.81 for the entire job, or barely eight cents per acre. Weatherford estimated that the 1C-12 saved him $600 in fuel costs alone over his previous year with his 60hp gasoline tractor.

As the success of Caterpillar's diesels became known, Art Rosen underwent celebrity status similar to that of Rudolf Diesel himself. Rosen delivered more than a dozen research papers between 1932 and 1935. Most significant to technical listeners and farmers alike were the performance characteristics of the diesel.

Rosen emphasized the engine's lugging ability. Its "rated load" was usually well below its peak load capacity. This gave operators a wide margin of power for a tough situation. Its torque curve most clearly exemplified the difference between gasoline engines and the diesel: reducing engine speed by 5 percent increased torque by 10 percent in the diesel. But this would improve gas engine torque by only 2 1/2 percent. On a practical basis, this meant that the diesel had superior ability to pull itself out of difficulty without greatly reducing engine speed to increase torque.

Of the first dozen Caterpillar diesels, two went to Hawaii to Theo H. Davies for the cane plantations. Art Rosen went with them. There, he soon learned that the heavier diesel crawler

OLIVER

The Oliver company dated back to 1868 when Scotsman James Oliver patented the chilled plow, so called because during the process of casting the iron, the outer surface is cooled more rapidly than the center. This gave the plow a harder finish. Oliver opened his shops in South Bend, Indiana in 1853 and by 1900 was widely known for other implements as well. In 1929, Oliver merged with Hart-Parr and several other companies to create Oliver Farm Equipment Corporation. Tractors were called Oliver Hart-Parr into the late thirties.

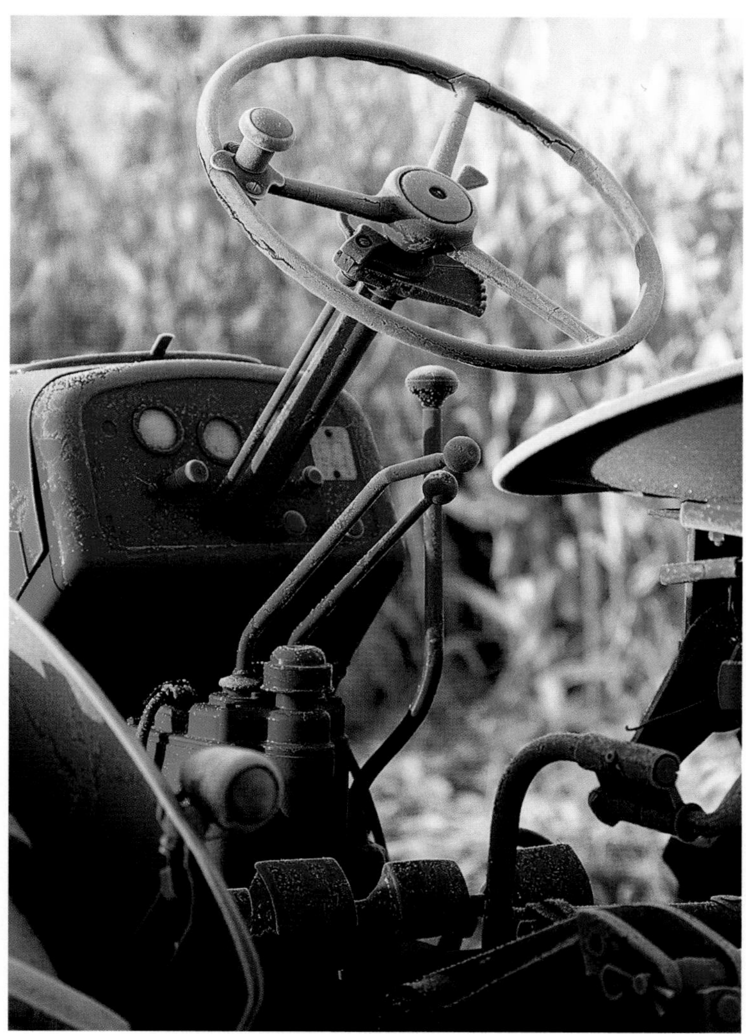

Power-adjustable rear wheels were an option popular with all manufacturers; Oliver sold theirs for $205. This 1954 diesel row-crop Super 66 sold for less than $3,300. Power steering was optional at $198. Both single and dual front row crop configurations were offered in addition to an adjustable wide front axle.

with no more horsepower than the gas model was actually less effective on the hillsides. To satisfy the operators, he had to open up the smoke screw (allowing more fuel into the mix). This was a trick quickly learned by many other engineers and mechanics after Rosen.

Another nine of the first two dozen went to Eygen-Bilsen, Belgium, in the spring of 1932. The job there was excavating the Albert Canal. The diesel seemed like the perfect solution to farmers', and even contractors', needs. But selling the diesel engine was difficult. With the money involved, no farmer or builder wanted to be first—or even early, for that matter—to jump on the trend.

The Oliver diesel was a four-cylinder vertical in-line engine with 3.31x3.75in bore and stroke for total capacity of 129.3ci. Nebraska tests yielded 17.7 drawbar and a maximum of 25.0 belt pulley horsepower at 1,600rpm. This tractor was restored and owned by the late Tiny Blom of Manilla, Iowa.

OLIVER
SUPER 66
DIESEL
66

◂ *Oliver introduced its Fleetline series in 1948, standardizing appearance and a number of parts in the replacements for the 60, 70, and 80 series, known as the 66, 77, and 88. The Super series followed in 1954, with 55, 66, 77, and 88 model tractors offering independent disk brakes, independent PTO, and an onboard live hydraulic system called Hydra-Lectric.*

The sales grew slowly. Caterpillar sold more diesels in 1936 than it had in the previous four years combined. Production was up to 1,000 diesel engines per month. The goal was set for 1,500 per month in 1937. Then came trouble.

Engine problems were occurring everywhere in the world. Piston rings stuck. Cylinder walls scored. Main bearings burnt up.

Caterpillar had about 3,000 diesels in the field by this time. Art Rosen observed that engines running in the western United States on West Coast oils—oils with a paraffin base rather than the asphaltic-based oils from the eastern oil fields—didn't have as much of a problem with rings sticking. It took a cooperative effort between Standard Oil of California and Caterpillar to solve the problem. G. B. Neely was the engineer who worked with Rosen to develop the first detergent oil. Standard called it "Delo." Caterpillar's diesels worked again. Within two years, every manufacturer had a diesel in its line-up. By 1960, diesels constituted nearly half of every tractor engine in production. By the 1990s, diesels are nearly all that is available in tractors.

501 WORKMASTER
OFFSET
Ford

▴Dwight Emstrom restored and owns this 1957 Model 501 Offset Workmaster Diesel. This tractor is fitted with a single-row cultivator. The offset is 8in to the operator's left of the tractor center line, for better visibility while using implements.

◂This series of tractors was manufactured from 1955 through 1962. It could be purchased with either a four- or five-speed transmission, with or without power take-off or hydraulic lift. It was also available with Ford's Select-O-Shift transmission that used the equivalent of ten gears to keep engine speed in its most efficient power ranges.

▸Ford's engine in the 501 was its own in-line four-cylinder with 3.56x3.60in bore and stroke for total capacity of 144ci. Compression ratio was 16.0:1 (where as the gas version was 7.5:1 and 8.84:1 for LPG). Ford's horsepower figures for the diesel version were 29.3 drawbar horsepower. Ford used the same 144ci engine in the 501, 601, and 701 series tractors.

▲*The Ford Dexta was equipped with a six forward-gear transmission that provided a top road speed of 17.3mph. The diesel Dexta weighed 3,393lb, but when ballasted up to nearly 6,000lb gross weight, the three-cylinder diesel was capable of pulling 4,362lb in first gear in tests at University of Nebraska.*

▸*Ford Motor Co., Ltd. of England, introduced the diesel-engined New Major model at a show in London in 1951 with deliveries starting in 1952. A 16:1 compression ratio was used. This 1958 Dexta model followed the New Major as a smaller companion in the mid-fifties. Ford in the U.S. introduced the diesel for 1958 models.*

Ford

4-17 CT

▲ *As early as 1948, Ford of England had offered the Perkins P6 diesel as an option to its Fordson Model E27N tractor. With fuel costs so much higher in England and Europe than in the United States, interest in economical diesel fuel led to healthy sales. But the Perkins was a stopgap effort. Factory engineers had began to develop a Ford diesel engine in 1944.*

◂ *The Dexta used Ford's three-cylinder 3.5x5.0in vertical engine. Total capacity was 144ci. It was tested at Nebraska in March 1959 and produced 23.0 drawbar horsepower and 31.4 maximum brake horsepower through the PTO at 2,000rpm. This English Ford is owned by Palmer Fossum of Northfield, Minnesota.*

▲*Frank Bettencourt's 1948 narrow-gauge D4 was first used in beet fields in California's Santa Clara Valley. It is fitted up to a John Deere-Killifer Model 7MKO-02 disk. Bettencourt, like many collectors, is gathering the implements used by the machines as well as the tractors themselves. The disk is scheduled for restoration.*

▸ *University of Nebraska tested a Caterpillar D4 in July 1949. In the tests, the four-cylinder 4.5x5.5in bore and stroke in-line diesel produced 33.0 drawbar and 46.5 belt pulley horsepower at 1,400rpm. The tractor weighed 11,175lb and in low gear was able to pull 9,555lb. The five-speed transmission offered a top speed of 5.4mph.*

▲*Bettencourt's D4 was fitted with an aftermarket live hydraulic system produced by Be-Ge Manufacturing Co. in Gilroy, California. By shifting the lever rising up behind the seat, the operator could raise or forcefully lower hydraulically assisted implements such as the Killifer disk.*

▸*It is an uncommon story of competitors helping in adversity. Massey-Ferguson's large tractor factory in Detroit suffered a serious fire in 1961, destroying its capacity to produce tractors. Negotiations with Oliver led to license and manufacture of its Model 990GM as the Massey Model 98 through 1962. This unusual 1962 machine belonged to the late Tiny Blom of Manilla, Iowa.*

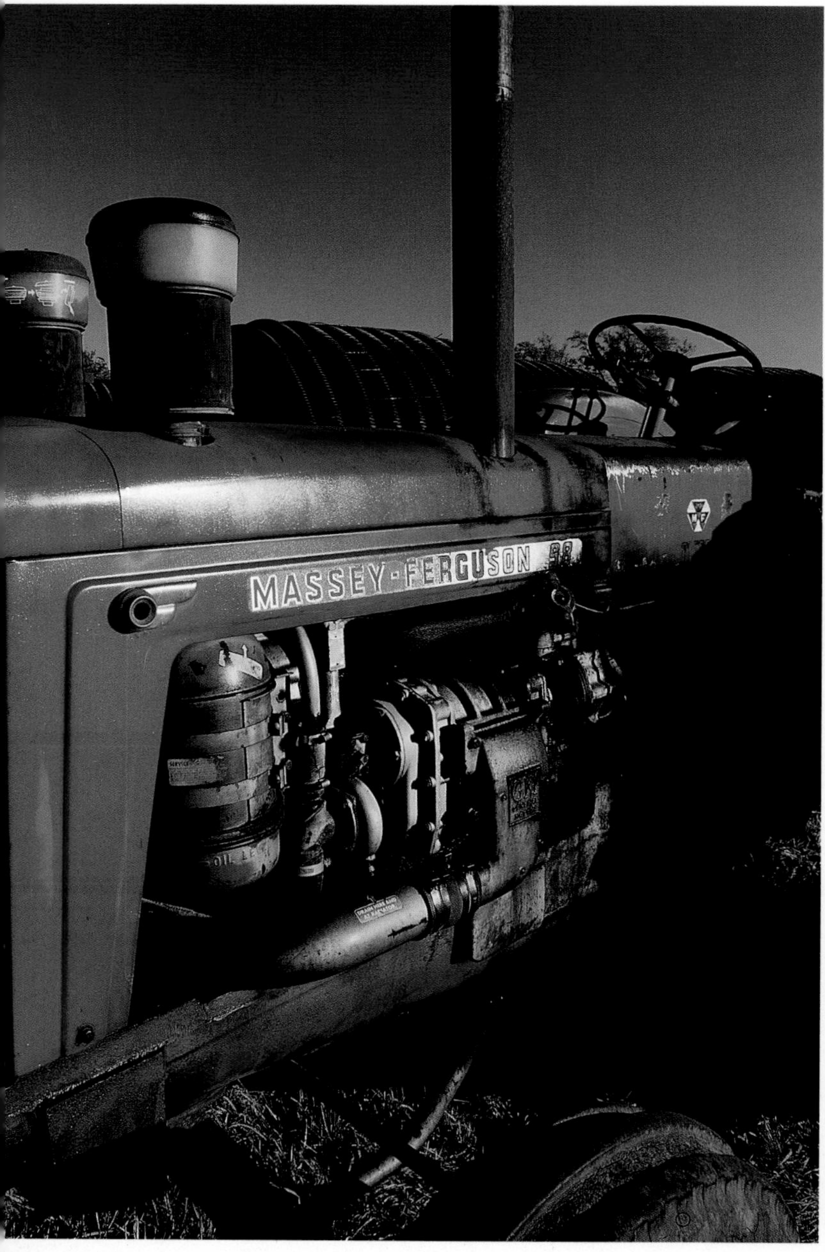

▲*Power for the Model 98 came from a General Motors 3-71 diesel three-cylinder in-line vertical engine fitted with a GMC supercharger. Bore and stroke was 4.25x5.0in for total capacity of 213ci. At 1,800rpm, the drawbar horsepower was rated at 61.6 and belt pulley output was 84.1hp. The large exhaust pipe, coupled with the supercharger howl, created a marvelous roar.*

▸*Iowa farmer and tractor collector Donald "Tiny" Blom specialized in collecting Oliver and Hart-Parr tractors. This Massey-Ferguson, with its Oliver parentage, was one of the more significant pieces of his agricultural machinery collection. An Oliver and Hart-Parr farmer for many years, he passed away in early 1995.*

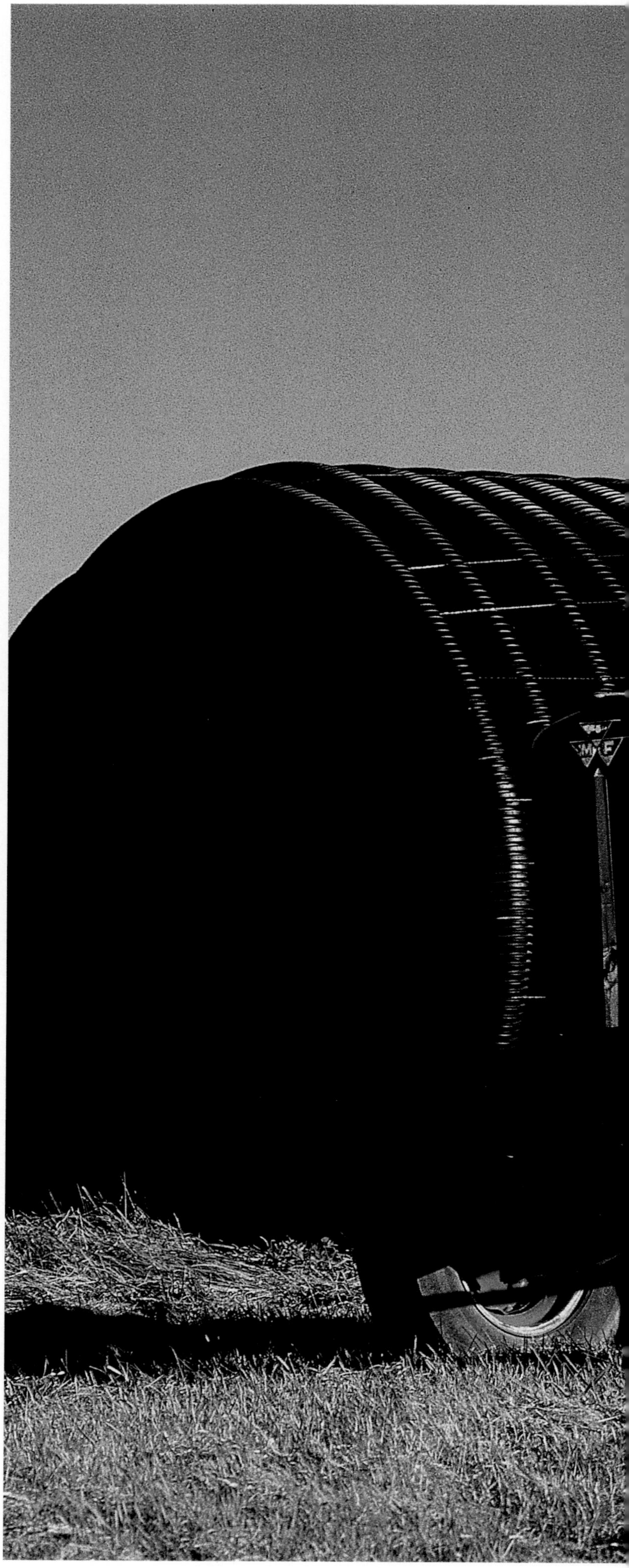

MASSEY-FERGUSON 98

Chapter Five

A Rubber Revelation

FIRESTONE AND ALLIS-CHALMERS TIRE THE INDUSTRY

AGRICULTURAL HISTORY MIGHT SUGGEST that persistence and nonconformity were daily marching orders to most tractor inventors. Such was the case with many managers as well. General Otto H. Falk was brought into Allis-Chalmers on April 16, 1913, to operate the company following its second courtship with bankruptcy in a decade. Falk was a retired Wisconsin National Guard brigadier who was neither a businessman nor a farmer. But lacking these two disciplines meant his imagination was unfettered.

His ideas were innovative; for example, his first tractor, a 10 to 18hp rated tricycle, was built on a one-piece, heat-treated steel frame. Allis-Chalmers' promotional literature boasted that "it has no rivets to work loose," that it "will not sag under the heaviest strains." But its single front wheel was offset; this made steering difficult under those same heavy loads. Falk's nonconformist designs kept early Allis-Chalmers tractors from being accepted or respected by the marketplace.

The second generation Falk tractor was the 6-12. It was conceived as a full-system machine that drove two large wheels far out front, beneath its engine. The implement-of-choice served as the rear-wheel assembly. That one too closely conformed to Moline Plow Company's Universal, and this prompted a note from Moline about patent infringement. By August 1923, Allis had dropped the 6-12. But whether it was discontinued because of Moline Plow's insistence or simply because of farmer disinterest is uncertain.

Ironically, Falk had succeeded back in December 1919. Allis-Chalmers brought to the market a stylish tractor with a 15 to 30hp rating. Its smart appearance suggested current automobile designs. Seen in profile, a continuous line ran from the radiator back to the fenders over the rear drive wheels and circled down nearly to the ground. Allis-Chalmers reclassified it in February 1920 as the 18-30.

▲*The Hercules Gas Engine Company of Evansville, Indiana, produced one-to-fourteen horsepower single-cylinder stationary engines for farm power from 1912 until 1934. Hercules Motors Corporation of Canton, Ohio, began producing four- and six-cylinder tractor and truck engines in 1915. It introduced a four-cylinder diesel in 1932. Hercules was owned by Hupp and then White Motor Corporation from 1961 through 1976.*

▸*Eagle Manufacturing Company was founded in 1888 in Appleton, Wisconsin. Beginning in 1899, they produced gasoline engines and in 1910 they made large, powerful tractors using their new two-cylinder and four-cylinder engines, followed in 1913 by a smaller model. Two-cylinder machines strongly resembling Waterloo Boy tractors remained in production until 1930 when Eagle began buying six-cylinder engines outside.*

But an accident of bad timing slowed the 18-30 to a complete halt within a couple of years of introduction. The economy had dug into a depression following World War I. Henry Ford had reacted to the sales slow down of his new Fordson by cutting its price by more than half. Those manufacturers who could afford to play along with Ford dropped their prices, too. But many of them who thought they could afford to price their tractors competitively—and many of those who knew they couldn't—went under. Allis-Chalmers sold only 235 of the Model 18-30 in 1920.

Allis introduced a similar but less muscular tractor, the 12-20, in 1921, but it suffered badly from the depression and the tractor price wars, selling only 1,705 up to 1928. Yet business resumed when the economy loosened up. General Falk had taken a beating during the first of his two decades with Allis-Chalmers. He force-fed tractors to a company onto which he had been forced. He had made mistakes in design and engineering, and those had cost Allis money, but he saw the future, and he knew that tractors would be there. Allis must have tractors to survive. So he persevered. By 1926, his favorite department was well-established. Tractor production grew twenty times as great in 1928 as it had been in 1926, with total sales nearing 16,000.

In 1926, Falk hired a bright talent, Harry C. Merritt. By all accounts, Merritt was a progressive innovator. He looked on the Allis-Chalmers' tractors from a similar perspective to Falk's—the view of the future. As Falk's tractor department manager, he was in a position to move the products; and with the department being clearly Falk's favorite son, Merritt received encouragement as well.

EAGLE·6

▲*Eagle used a Hercules Model QXB-5 in-line six-cylinder engine of 3.25x4.125in bore and stroke. Eagle rated it at 18.0 drawbar and 28.0 belt pulley horsepower at 1,575 rpm. A Zenith carburetor and a Splitdorf HT magneto were standard equipment. The Model 6C weighed 3,250lb, and measured 69in tall, 66in wide, and 130in overall.*

▸*Eagle introduced its 6C, the Utility, in 1938. Four gears allowed top road speed of 13mph. Auto-Lite electrics provided starting and lights. This is tractor No. 2,494, and Eagle's numbers stop at 2,500. By 1939, Eagle was selling off inventory, and the company disappeared by 1940. This tractor was restored and is owned by Walter and Bruce Keller of Kaukauna, Wisconsin.*

The new Allis-Chalmers Model 20-35 was introduced in 1929, three years after Merritt's arrival. This was a slightly improved version of its predecessor, the 18-30. Also known as the Model L, it was available for only two years. Meanwhile, Allis prepared a new tractor for an outside marketing firm, United Tractor and Equipment (UT&E) of Chicago.

This was to be a three-plow rated machine, using a four-cylinder Continental engine. When UT&E failed—despite seemingly adequate outside support and backing—Allis continued to produce its tractor, marketing it as the Model U.

In the spring of 1929, Merritt traveled west, visiting California in May. He was startled and impressed by the wild poppies that covered the hillsides like bright blankets. Their brilliant orange color struck him.

Returning to Milwaukee, he faced the somber green tractors produced by his department. Allis-Chalmers tractors were invisible in the green fields across North America. He felt his products—improving with every successive model—should stand out against the green of growing crops, and against the other makers' somber colors. "Persian" orange most closely matched the wild meadows of California. It wasn't long before Merritt's orange tractors dotted the fields.

Allis-Chalmers' tractor marketing efforts were given a huge boost with the acquisition in 1931 of the Advance-Rumely Thresher Co. This purchase accomplished what General Falk had not succeeded at doing on his own. Overnight, Advance-Rumely provided Allis-Chalmers with a well-established dealer organization that sold a highly respected line of tractors and implements. Allis' Model U remained in production through 1944, and Allis built more than 10,000 of them. Continental engines powered early Model Us until Allis-Chalmers' own UM four-cylinder engine appeared in 1933. This tractor was offered in a

▲ *Production of the Row Crop tricycle began in March 1930 and was up to twenty units a day by April. The single-front wheel was replaced with a dual-front beginning in 1932. In 1937, this same model became the Oliver 80, on rubber tires. This original, unrestored 1931 machine was owned by the late Tiny Blom of Manilla, Iowa.*

◄ *The Row Crop sold new for $985. Oliver inaugurated its advertising campaign promoting "Power on Tiptoe" with this model. Its narrow rims were fitted with solid iron grousers. The point of these wheels—and of Oliver's advertising—was to emphasize the limited soil compaction caused by these rear, load-bearing wheels.*

variety of styles, including an "Ind-U-strial" model, a crawler, a railroad yard switcher built by Brookville Locomotive, and a row-crop version.

But it was not only its longevity, its adaptability, or even its new color for which Allis-Chalmer's Model U is most famous. It was for Harry Merritt's friendship with Harvey Firestone.

In his 1951 history, *The Firestone Story*, Alfred Lief categorized Firestone's relationship with Allis as one of the Firestone Company's "self-helps to recovery" from the financial depression following the war. It was that at the very least.

Firestone's family farm, the Homestead in Columbiana, Ohio, about fifteen miles south of Youngstown, ran on steel and was operated with Allis-Chalmers tractors. Harry Merritt had of-

▲ *The Hart-Parr in-line four-cylinder engine measured 4.125x5.25in bore and stroke. At 700rpm, it produced 18.0 drawbar horsepower and a peak of 29.7 belt pulley horsepower in its tests in April 1930 at University of Nebraska. Oliver fitted a Bosch U4 magneto and Ensign Model K carburetor which was protected behind a large Donaldson air cleaner. The tractor weighed 4,650lb.*

▲*Beginning in 1930, Allis-Chalmers engineers field tested pre-production models of its new Model U fitted with rubber tires on a farm near Waukesha, Wisconsin, belonging to Albert Schroeder. The tests were very successful. Nebraska's board of governors heard about the Allis-Chalmers/Firestone development and invited Allis-Chalmers to bring a rubber-tired Model U for a test, waiving the usual $500 test fee.*

▸*Allis-Chalmers designed the tractor for the United Farmers Cooperative who were then unable to put the machine into production. An Allis-Chalmers United was tested at Nebraska in November 1929 on steel. Using the Continental four-cylinder 4.25x5.0in engine, 19.3 drawbar and 35.0 pulley horsepower were recorded. The 4,821lb tractor pulled 3,679lb in low gear.*

fered Firestone one of the company's new Model U tractors. Firestone, long convinced of the value of pneumatic tires for cars and trucks on the road, wondered about their application to the farm. Surely, for the more than a million farm tractors in use on steel wheels, the same economy of operation, the same operator comfort, the same reduction in vibration would apply—if the problem of traction could be solved.

Firestone understood the conditions. The ground and crop clearance required of a tractor in all farm operations demanded that the tire have a large diameter and a wide cross section for contact with the soil. Yet it still had to fit within the furrow. Contact with the soil had to be firm so the tractor would pull; however, too much air pressure would pack the soil too hard. Yet the grip could not be so great, or the pressure so little, that the tire would creep on the rim.

Firestone's engineers tried flat truck rims first. Airplane tires were mounted on them, but they rim-crept. The answer was a drop-center rim with a tight bead fit. So much for creepage. As for traction, the tread had to bite into earth, sand, wet clay, or sod. However, if they were cut too deep or had insufficient support, the treads could bend under the load. The engineers modified a chevron pattern, inventing a connected bar design, the continuation of one side of the chevron to the bar above it. With Firestone himself at the wheel, the engineers settled on 12 to 15psi for tire inflation.

Firestone's farm was completely re-tired; each tractor and implement—thirty-two in all—was changed over to his new "Ground Grip" pneumatic tire. Merritt changed the specifications on his Model U. Inflatable rubber was offered as an option. To promote some of the virtues of the new tires that were introduced for general sale in January 1935, Firestone and Merritt

▲*The tire paint is fading but the history is clear. This is a replica of the first tractor tested on rubber tires at the University of Nebraska. It was fitted with 6.50x20 rayon Firestone Transport Heavy-Duty Truck-Bus eight-ply tires on the front and 11.25x24in airplane tires on the rear. French & Hecht manufactured the rims. This replica belongs to the University of Nebraska tractor test museum and it is photographed on the concrete test track that rubber tires eventually made necessary.*

▶*Five years later, The Model U was tested on rubber and again on steel. While Allis-Chalmers had begun making its own engine, test results with the same tractor on steel and on rubber revealed dramatic benefits to rubber tires. A four-hour fuel economy run produced 6.14 horsepower hours per gallon with 16.9 drawbar horsepower on steel, and 8.57 at 22.7hp on rubber. None of that even began to demonstrate the improvement in operator comfort.*

coaxed Indianapolis racer Barney Oldfield out of retirement. They put him back on the county fair race circuit, on a rubber-shod Model U. *Implement & Tractor* magazine reported that countless events were run. In five lap races against local Allis owners and salesmen, Oldfield let the amateurs lead for the first four laps, then he would sprint past them, showing off the ultimate speed and traction capabilities of the Allis-Chalmers rubber-tired combination. Merritt fitted especially high "road" gears to the racers; on one top speed run, Oldfield set a record of better than 64mph with a specially modified U and Firestone's tires.

The brightly colored rubber-shod tractors garnered a lot of attention, even as farmers acknowledged the uselessness of 64mph machines. The Model U became the first tractor in North America available with rubber. When Merritt introduced Allis' second-generation row-crop, the WC in 1934, it was the first tractor to be designed with inflatable rubber tires specified as standard equipment. Firestone's Super Grip Type R tire improved the connected bar design. It provided greater depth, narrower width, and wider spacing between bars. These entered the soil more effectively and cleaned themselves on exit.

Lester Larsen, head of the tractor testing program at the University of Nebraska for thirty years, recalled that Allis-Chalmers had a Model U on Firestone rubber tires testing for a full year on Albert Schroeder's farm in Wisconsin. At the beginning of 1934, there were only three tests scheduled, a Farmall F-12, a John Deere Model A, and Allis-Chalmers' new Model WC. The University of Nebraska Tractor Test Board of Governors had heard about the tire test in Wisconsin and about work on a Case Model C with Goodyear. The board extended an invitation to IHC, Deere, and Allis-

A-C
ALLIS-CHALMERS

PLYMOUTH

◂*The tiny 1934 Plymouth measured 49in tall (60in to the top of the steering wheel), 48in wide, and 100in long overall. Its wheelbase was 61in, its non-adjustable track width was 38in, and it ran 5.50x16 front tires and 9.5x24 rears. This unusual one-plow tractor is owned by Paul Brecheisen of Helena, Ohio.*

▴*Built by Fate-Root-Heath (FRH) Company of Plymouth, Ohio, the Plymouth tractor was named after the company's home town. FRH used a Hercules in-line four-cylinder Model IXA engine. In 1935, FRH renamed their tractors the Silver King line that continued in production until the late fifties.*

Chalmers to bring their tractors not only on steel but also to bring one—at no extra charge—on the rubber tires. Tests at that time cost the manufacturer $500. Only Allis-Chalmers accepted. During the test, the WC on steel produced 14.4 maximum drawbar horsepower. While on rubber, the same tractor produced 19.6hp and returned a 25 percent increase in fuel economy.

But people are often cautious and sometimes cruel toward new ideas. Where a farmer appeared with rubber tires on his tractor working the field, neighbors stood at the fence and called him "sissy," looking down their noses at the gentle ride. To placate the conservative farmers, steel wheels were still optional, up through the 1940 introduction of the WF standard tread version of the WC. Of course, World War II returned some of the U, WC, and WF models to steel out of necessity. But once the war ended, steel wheels were no longer available on these tractors. Farmers came to understand that while comfort may be sissified, the improved economy and performance definitely were not.

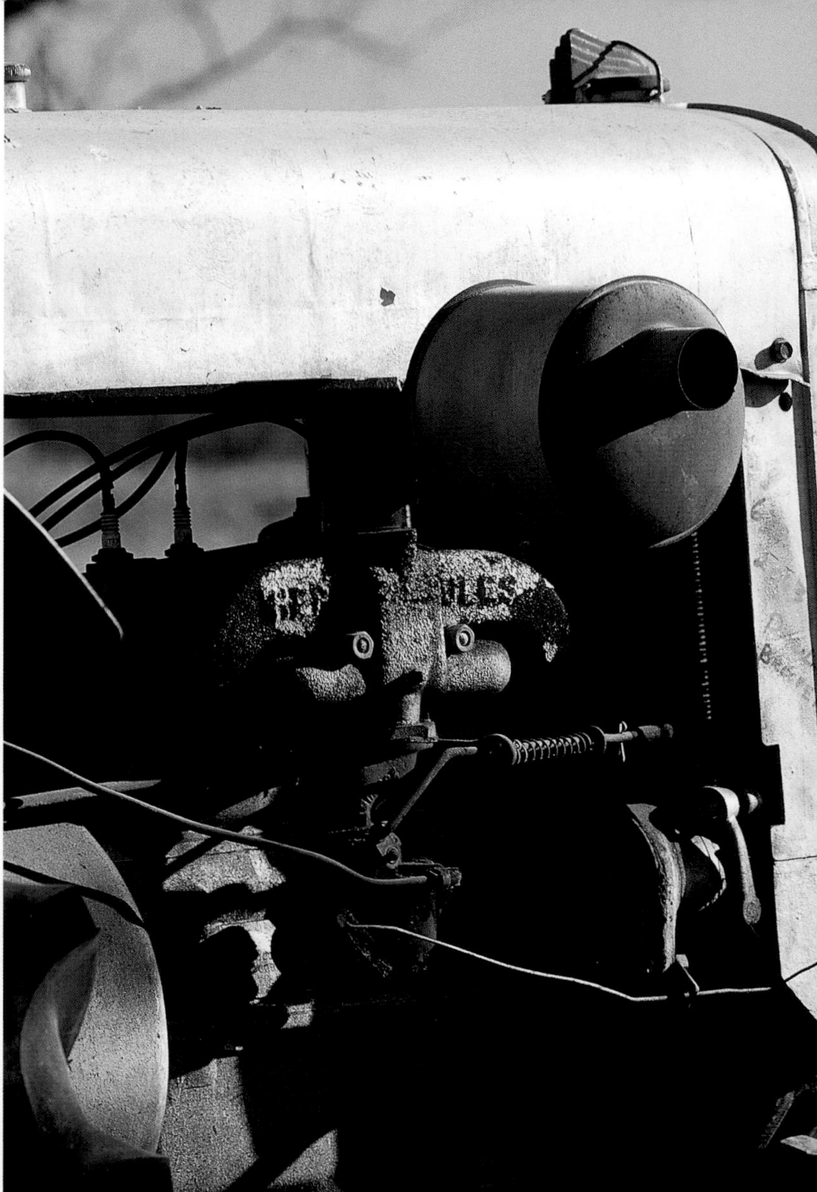

▲*The Hercules IXA engine measured 3.0x4.0in bore and stroke. The Plymouth used a Zenith 0.875in diameter carburetor as well as a Fairbanks-Morse magneto (although an International Harvester Corporation magneto has replaced the original Fairbanks unit on this version.) Horsepower was quoted as 10 on the drawbar and 20 on the belt pulley at 1,400rpm.*

◂*Fate-Root-Heath used a four-speed transmission offering a top road speed of 25mph. FRH built 325 Plymouths before renaming their tractors the Silver King. This was the 39th model manufactured. Plymouths were offered on either steel wheels or pneumatic rubber tires.*

ALLIS-CHALMERS

▲*This UC used Allis-Chalmer's own 4.375x5.0in bore and stroke in-line four-cylinder Model UM engine. It recorded maximum drawbar output at 18.9hp at 1,200rpm. Belt pulley power was 33.5hp. Rubber-tired versions could hit 10mph in fourth gear.*

◂*When the University of Nebraska tested the Allis-Chalmers Model U on both steel wheels as well as rubber tires, it also tested a new Model UC. Fuel economy was 5.35 horsepower hours per gallon on steel while it jumped to 8.96 on Firestone rubber.*

▲One significant feature of Allis-Chalmers tractors was the Snap-Coupler quick-attachment system for implements, which worked especially well with cultivators and similar attachments. Mounted under the tractor between the axles, these reportedly could be fitted or removed in less than five minutes for either operation. This 1937 model is owned by Conrad Schoessler of Westside, Iowa.

▸Allis-Chalmers introduced the Model UC in 1930, and it competed head-to-head with the Farmall Regular. The UC remained in production from 1930—using a Continental engine—through the 1934 introduction of their own Model UM engine until production was ended in 1941.

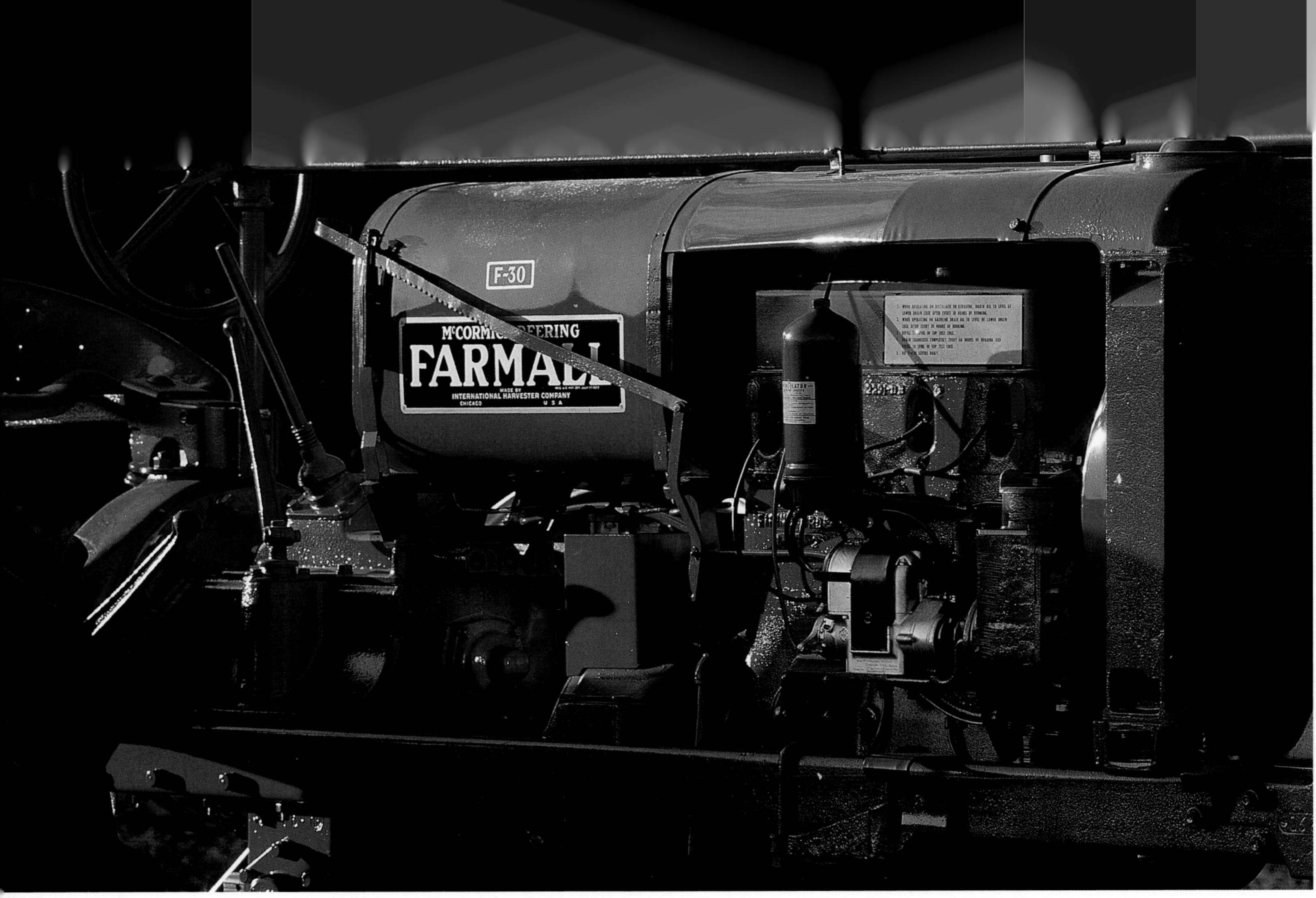

▲International Harvester manufactured its own in-line four-cylinder engines. This one measured 4.25x5.0in bore and stroke. In its Nebraska test in October 1931, it produced 24.9hp on drawbar at 1,150rpm, and 32.8 belt pulley horsepower.

◄The Model F-30 high clearance offered 27in of ground clearance below the drawbar. It stood 99in tall (81in to the top of the air cleaner) and 84in wide as well as 145in overall. This 1937 model is owned by Bob Pollock of Denison, Iowa.

►IHC used its own F4 magneto as well as a Zenith carburetor. The high clearance versions were designed specifically for use in sugar cane fields. This tractor sold new for around $1,225. Front tires were 8.0x21, rears were 13.6x44.

►►The Farmall-30, or F-30, was introduced in late 1931, and it remained in production until 1939. Its 94in wheelbase allowed a 17ft-4in turning circle. More than 28,000 Model F-30 tractors were produced.

FARMALL

F-30
McCORMICK-DEERING
FARMA

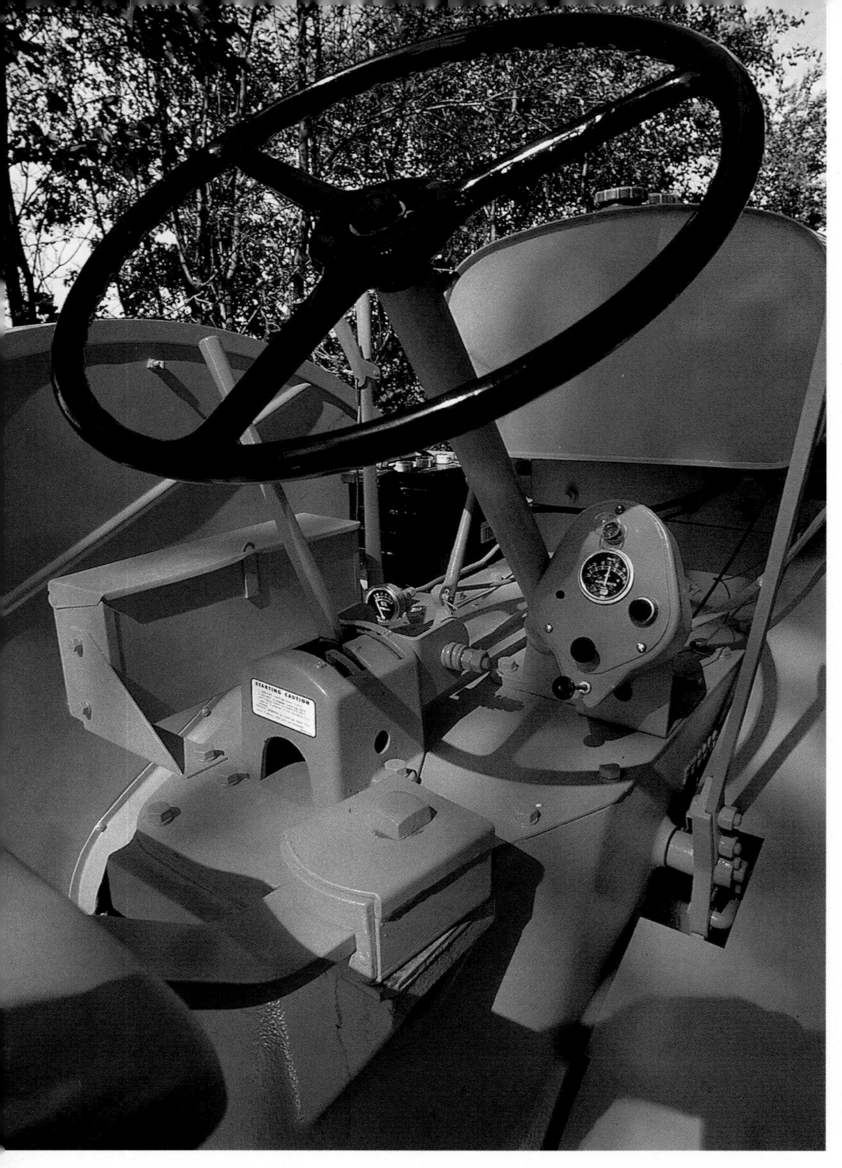

◂ *The Model G was introduced in 1940 as Minneapolis-Moline's strongest, heaviest tractor. For the 1942 model year, slight changes were made which allowed it to be renamed the GTA, as it continued to be called through 1946. On steel wheels it weighed around 7,100lb. It used a four-speed transmission with a top speed of 6mph whereas the rubber-tired versions had a fifth gear capable of 13.8mph.*

▸ *Due to U.S. government needs for rubber during World War II, the few tractors that were delivered during the War were only available on steel. These steel wheels measured 6.0x37in front and 12.0x50in rears with 5in grousers. This tractor is owned by Walter and Bruce Keller of Kaukauna, Wisconsin. It is a 1946 Model GTA.*

▾ *Minneapolis-Moline built its own in-line vertical four-cylinder engine for the G. This had bore and stroke of 4.625x6.0in. and total capacity of 403.2ci. A Marvel-Schebler carburetor was used along with a Delco generator and electric system. No tests were performed at University of Nebraska during the War but in 1950, a G on rubber tires was tested, producing 39.2 drawbar and 55.9 belt pulley horsepower at 1,100rpm.*

MINNEAPOLIS-MOLINE

CASE

▲*For an additional $55, buyers received rear fenders, the operator's platform, and the swinging drawbar. The stakes that protrude from the bottom of the rear fenders scraped grass and dirt from between the steel wheel grousers. The tractor was also available from as early as 1929 on hard rubber tires for industrial applications. Inflatable rubber came in 1934, at a price of $1,405 compared to $1,175 for the tractor on all steel wheels.*

◀*Connie Schoessler's 1927 Model L Case hugs the hillside on his Westside, Iowa, farm. Prior to the introduction of the Model L, many of Case's gasoline or kerosene-fueled tractors had their engines mounted transversely, or "cross-mounted". This model sold new for $1,295.*

◂The Case weighed 5,307lb and in first gear it pulled 4,555lb. The company offered the tractor with a three-speed transmission up until 1937 when four-speeds could be ordered on industrial and agricultural models. Top speed for the agricultural version on steel was 4mph; for either version on rubber, top speed was not quite 12mph.

▴Tested in Nebraska in 1929, the Model L did better than its advertised 26-40 rating. The four-cylinder 4.625x6.0in engine produced 30.0 drawbar and 44.0 belt pulley horsepower at 1,100rpm. Case fitted a Kingston L-3 carburetor and a Robert Bosch FU4 magneto.

Chapter Six

Fuel Evolution

Fractions Are Not Always Arithmetic

Liquefied petroleum gas—LPG—was just a waste gas. Before its commercial value was recognized, it had nicknames: "wet gas," "greased air," "fizz gas," and "overhead reflux." But once a market was created for it, it was proudly, and profitably, sold as Gasol and Gasolite, Pyrofax and Pyrogene, Readygas and Flamo, Skelgas, Shellane, and Bu-Gas. Generically, it was known as propane and butane.

It had been "discovered" by Dr. William O. Snelling, a thirty-one-year-old consulting chemist on the staff of the U.S. Geological Survey working in the explosives laboratory in Washington. Snelling succeeded in liquefying natural gas and storing it in a thick glass bowl. He lit the vapor above the liquid and used this flaming vapor to light his office for months before ever saying a word about it to anyone. He described the gas in rather technical terms to William Altdorfer, a freelance writer for the *Indianapolis Star*.

"The gas is prepared from 'heavy' natural gas, particularly waste gas which accumulates in the pipes of oil wells," Altdorfer learned in 1912 from his interview with Snelling. "The natural gas is compressed and cooled and the heavy fractions which condense are separated. The lighter fractions are next condensed and are forced under pressure into a vessel called the 'rectifier' where they come in contact with coils of super-heated steam and are completely vaporized. The gases then pass in succession through a series of coils, each heated to a lower temperature than the preceding one, and these coils separate the gas into a series of products...The higher compounds of the paraffin series of hydrocarbons—to which the chemical names of 'ethane,' 'propane' and 'butane' have been given—are liquefied."

In chemical terms, "fractioning" refers to separating the various elements of any mixture by distillation or crystallization processes. The success of these processes relies on the fact that each element has a different boiling point or solubility that allows its separation from other elements.

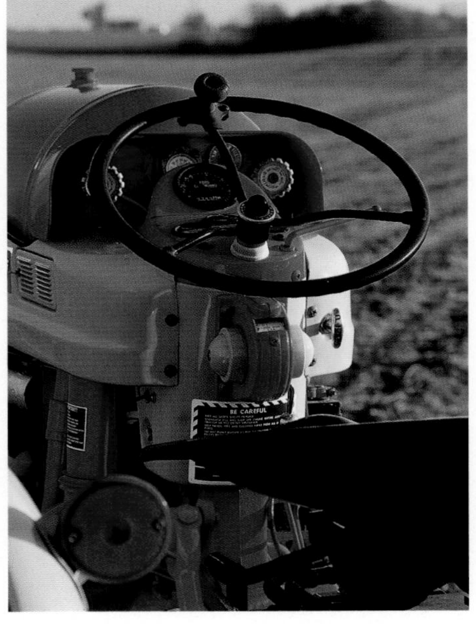

▲*Close to rocket science, the operator's view is an eyeful. A fuel level overflow valve and fuel gauge are just ahead of the standard 971 instrument panel. Below the panel is the controller for the Select-O-Speed transmission that indicates engine speeds at 1,200, 1,750 and 2,200rpm matched to gears to yield ground speeds from 0.6mph up to 18mph. Dwight Emstrom of Galesburg, Illinois, restored and owns this 1961 tractor.*

▸*The 971 stood 66in tall to the top of the instrument panel, 72in wide, and 133in long overall on its 85in wheelbase. Ready for work with water ballasted tires and LPG equipment it weighed about 5,970lb, roughly 100lb more than the same tractor burning gasoline. Front tires were 5.50-16in duals while rears were 12.0-28s. Ground clearance was 27.5in.*

If this entire operation sounds much like the working procedures of steam engines or even early gasoline, coal dust, and diesel engines, there is some similarity. A vapor, gas in this case, is cooled and condensed to liquid, whereupon it is heated and expanded into vapor form again, after which it is once again condensed. But this last condensation is done extremely slowly and deliberately. This will separate the various flammable elements from the original liquid or its vapor.

As early as 1860, Julius Pintsch, a German, developed a compressed gas for high temperature oil processes. But it was fifty years later, in 1901, that another German chemist, Hermann Blau, invented a process to liquefy petroleum gas. Patented in the United States in 1904, Blau gas had a foul aroma, but it was used as cooking and lighting fuel. Blau's patent covered bottling it for widespread distribution. It could be sold in shops like so many food stuffs.

Between 1905 and 1910, several LPG pioneers established businesses to deal with separating, storing, and marketing the wet, greasy gases. Frank Peterson of Mercer, Pennsylvania, extracted gas from anthracite coal in 1905, which he then used as fuel for his own small engines. In 1909, Andy and Chester Kerr formed Riverside Oil Company in Pittsburgh, Pennsylvania, to produce natural gas. In the next two years, Riverside built twenty gas plants and launched the boom. In 1912, more than a thousand new plants opened in western Pennsylvania and Virginia.

Gasoline, a hydrocarbon fuel, had experienced a huge surge in demand at the

FORD 971 SELECT-O-SPEED

FORD 971 SELECT O SPEED

◂ *Live power-take-off was provided by use of a double clutch that kept PTO power engaged even when the tractor was stopped. The swinging drawbar was designed to function fully without interfering with either the PTO or the hydraulic three-point hitch system. Rear wheel tread width could be adjusted by engine power in 0.5in increments from 56in to 84in.*

beginning the century, due to the increasing promotion of gas-engine automobiles and the development of the gasoline engine tractor. Refining crude oil or petroleum into gasoline requires a series of distillations of the product. This is sometimes called cracking, a decomposition process by heat and pressure that breaks molecules down to form simpler ones of lower boiling point. Each successive step further controls the quality and purity of the product. Because of the repetition necessary, gasoline always remained more costly than gas-oil distillates, kerosene, and other products obtained from the first distillation, or straight-run, process. Blended gasoline, even more costly yet, could provide specific properties; for example, about ten percent of the mixture may be a low boiling point material that would vaporize without heat on the manifold, as is the case when an engine is started the first time on a cold day.

Robert Clay, the managing editor of *Butane-Propane News*, wrote a fifty-year history of the LPG industry in 1962. His interview with industry founder Andy Kerr was entertaining.

Clay set the scene of the early days in his own, vivid writing style: "The gasoline obtained from these plants was an ornery, dangerous product," he wrote. "It contained a considerable volume of petroleum gases that boiled out of the liquid whether it was in storage, in transit, or in use. A. N. Kerr once rather colorfully and modestly described his side of this situation: 'I deserve no credit for being the first to plunge into the sale of butane and propane. I tried in every way to avoid selling these products. I tried to pass them on to the gasoline trade, but they boiled out of our casing-head gasoline and splashed red ink all over our ledger. These liquid gases made our works at Sistersville so dangerous that we were compelled to build high waste lines with Christmas tree outlets [dump and drainage lines that spread out like the branches of a tree] in order to avoid having an excess of dangerous gas float over the Baltimore & Ohio railroad main line adjoining the works [where it could be ignited by a stray steam engine spark with horrifying results]. I was literally forced to put this gas in its proper place. A daily loss of 1,400 gallons (of vaporized gases) at that time amounted to approximately $150 and no Scotchman could overlook that.'"

But capturing and controlling the vapor was where its orneriness and danger came in. Herman Stukeman, one of Andy Kerr's young engineers, filed a report on the Kerrs' Riverside efforts on Christmas Eve 1910. "While we were condensing the first liquid, our gas line broke and filled the room to a depth of one foot with gas. Apparently the gas did not have enough air mixed with it to burn, except above the one-foot depth. Two helpers in the engine room—who, as helpers will do, were watching the boss repair the leak—had rings burned around their trousers one foot from the floor; otherwise, they were untouched.

"The supervisor [Andy Kerr] being in the fire zone and on his knees, had within the week a new and thinner skin on his face and hands. On retiring from the room, as all did promptly, the gas was observed to be burning from the top, about twelve inches from the floor. No harm was done except to the complexion.

971 SELECT-O-SPEED

▲*The engine of the gas and kerosene tractors was the same except for a dual-fuel carburetor. The four-cylinder engine of 3.19x3.75in bore and stroke produced 14.9 drawbar horsepower at a fuel economy of 8.8 horsepower hours per gallon of tractor fuel. The gasoline version produced 17.7 drawbar horsepower at 10.13 horsepower hours per gallon of fuel. The advantage of kerosene was simply that it sold for about half the price of gasoline.*

►*The "A" in the model designation 8N-AN stands for "all fuel" or "tractor fuel." Dual filler caps separated one from the other. This dual-fuel Ford belongs to Palmer Fossum of Northfield, Minnesota. In June 1950, an all-fuel Ford 8N and a gasoline 8N were tested at University of Nebraska, revealing significant differences in performance and economy. This is a 1952 version.*

◄*The LPG tank holds 24gal with a buffer for fuel to expand as it heats up during a routine work day. The gas is fed through a filter, vaporizer, and regulator before reaching the carburetor. The four-cylinder engine measured 3.90in bore and 3.60in stroke for total engine capacity of 172ci. Power output was rated at approximately 43.0 drawbar and 50.0 belt pulley horsepower.*

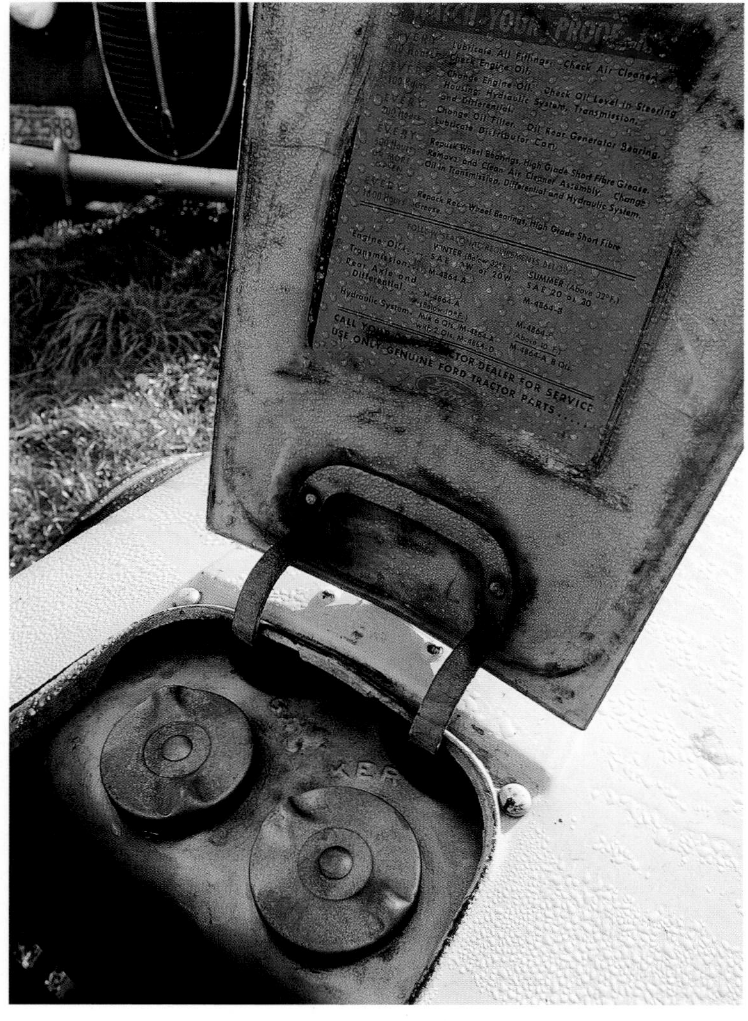

"After our fire experience," Stukeman concluded with understatement, "we had considerable respect for this gas.... (From then on) we used welded containers and gas regulators and reduced the gas to low pressures."

Independently—and in much greater safety—research chemist Snelling had determined through scientific experiments what Andy Kerr had learned painfully: that liquefied petroleum gas was a mixture of propane, butane, pentane, and other separated gas mixture elements.

Still, the dangers were not past. A few months later, one of Kerr's employees at their Sistersville plant was frozen by escaping butane and died. Through fire and ice, each passing horror ex-

MINNEAPOLIS
MOLINE
MINNEAPOLIS
MOLINE
MINNEAPOLIS
G704

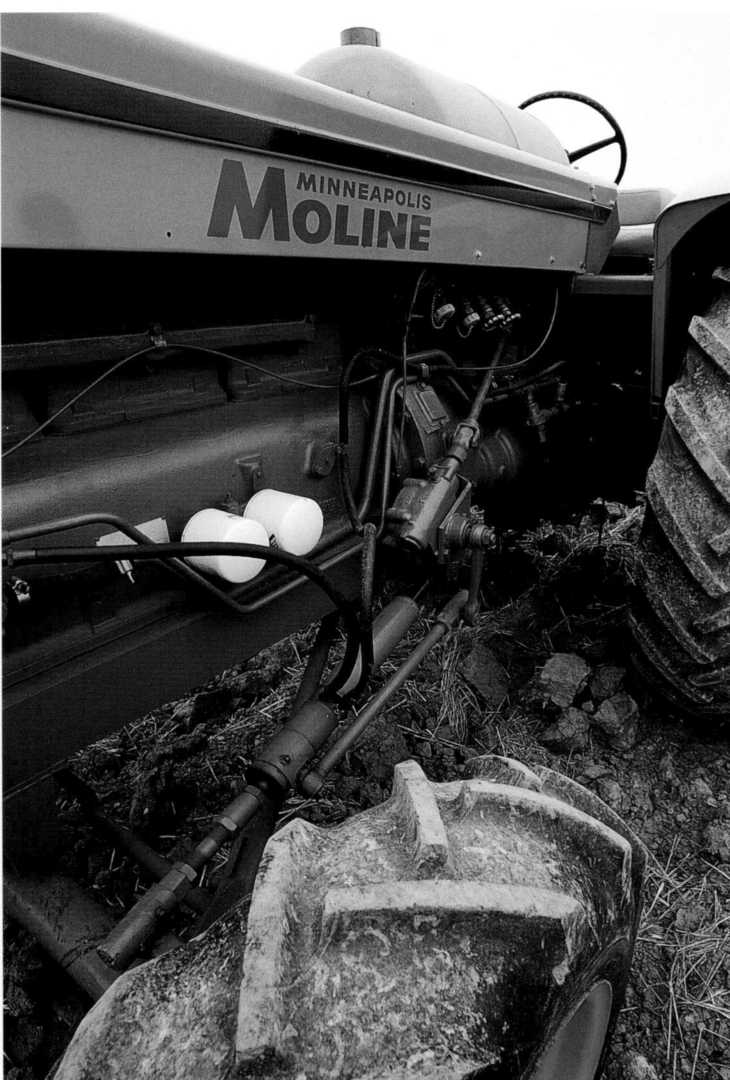

▲*In an indication of the move to alternate fuels, Minneapolis-Moline (M-M) offered this tractor only with diesel or LPG fuel. The six-cylinder 4.25x5.0in bore and stroke engine provided a total capacity of 425ci. At 1,500rpm, Minneapolis-Moline rated the tractor at 82hp on the PTO. Fuel capacity is 41gal of LPG. With its Ellwood mechanical front wheel drive system, it was rated as a nine-plow tractor.*

◂*The G704 stands 96in tall to the top of the muffler, 76in wide, and 151in long overall on a 85in wheelbase. In LPG configuration, it weighs 8,550lb. Top road speed in 5th gear is 17.1mph. It operated on 9.2x24in 4-ply front tires and 18.4x36 6-ply rears. Power-steering was standard equipment. Bruce Keller operated the 1962 heavy-weight near his home in Kaukauna, Wisconsin.*

panded the body of knowledge. Snelling joined the Kerrs in late 1911, and together they founded American Gasol, the name Chester Kerr had given to the propane fraction a year before. Two years later, they were all bought out by E.W. DeBower, the founder of America's most successful home study programs, LaSalle Extension Course. DeBower had done his homework. He learned a great deal about the economic potential of the gases. He offered the partners $50,000 for their company, and all but Snelling were glad to be out of the risky, if suddenly profitable, business.

Development continued. During World War I, Dr. J. B. Garner of Hope Natural Gas Company in Pittsburgh, Pennsylvania, introduced the word "butane" to consumers. Garner worked to improve its image. Nicknamed "greasy air," the gas had been previously promoted for industrial uses; many chemists and engineers still thought it was too risky for home use, despite the fact that butane had successfully powered an automobile in 1912. But by 1920, the Kerrs, back in the business again, had concluded that the greasy air would "work very well in practically any gasoline-type burner." In 1922, LPG sales totaled 223,000 gallons nationwide. And the Kerr brothers, in from the beginning, sparked LPG's next big flash.

Andy Kerr moved to Long Beach, California, and set up the Imperial Gas Company in 1925. As he explained later to editor Robert Clay, "It was thought that the Imperial Valley [a desert farming area in Southern California between Indio and El Centro] would be a good market. The first set—a revaporizing kind of wet gas outfit—was too expensive, as it consisted of two regulators, one of which used liquid, and it had three tanks...While this plant would use any type of cheap product, it sold for $125." Not cheap in 1925.

When Kerr concluded that this was far too costly for the California farmers, he simplified the package into the first successful tank-vapor system using one tank and one regulator. This was intended for home heating and cooking, and Kerr was assisted by both Standard Oil Company of California and by Shell Oil Company, which was poised to introduce its own propane-propylene mixture, Shellane. Standard's Long Beach-based Lomita Oil Company soon brought out Readygas, which it test marketed and introduced as Flamo. And Phillips Petroleum, at that time the largest natural gas producer, began to examine the challenges, logistics, and value in transporting liquefied petroleum gases by rail to distributors around the United States. As home owners in rural areas began to accept butane and propane for home heating and cooking uses, the manufacturers continued working out the kinks in the hardware.

Clay described an ongoing struggle: "It was not uncommon for domestic sets to lose many pounds of fuel each day. Because LPG not only operated under higher pressure, but also had pronounced solvent qualities, the loose fits, rubber compounds, and grease packing that worked with natural gas would not work very long with LPG." Yet even as the chemists and researchers, tinkerers, and inventors struggled with these problems, other individuals sought out new uses for the fuels.

Standard Oil had established Lomita Oil in 1923, pumping gas and fractioning it from its pumps and fields on Signal Hill at the north end of the city of Long Beach. Sometime in 1928, as Lomita began to promote the commercial uses of propane and butane, Charles McCartney, a Stanford University engineering dropout, walked in the front door with an idea. McCartney believed that either of the two gases could be used as motor fuels. He asked Lomita to put him in business distributing gas for this virtually untapped market. He quickly founded Petrolane and set out selling butane as an engine fuel to farmers from El Centro to Bakersfield.

At that time, in 1928, Los Angeles-based George Holzapfel—among others—had begun work to develop LPG carburetors. A year later, Shell had a truck in its fleet testing the fuel daily. In 1930, due in part to McCartney's vision, Standard of California announced that 127 of its salesmen would be driving its Flamo-powered trucks. As Clay pointed out, Flamo was propane, and the large Standard Oil program produced a huge butane by-product surplus.

This was, of course, a time of boom and bust. McCartney was selling a conversion that cost $150 to $250 for a farm tractor. But once it was converted, the tractor ran on fuel that cost four or five cents a gallon compared to eighteen cents for gasoline. In addition, butane burned so much cleaner that routine maintenance such as oil changes could be stretched to nearly double the engine running time. Furthermore, butane, as a fuel, simply produced more power than gasoline. Other inventors and manufacturers joined as outside suppliers to the volatile market. Still others enlisted as inventors-turned-disciples.

Roy Hansen, a licensed mechanical and civil engineer in Lomita, was in business manufacturing carburetors and tanks in 1933. He formed an alliance with Petrolane, and Hansen and McCartney began traveling north to Stockton and Sacramento and beyond to find new customers and new distributors.

Converting tractors—in the early days these were largely Caterpillars—was not extremely difficult, though it was involved and it did require some internal engine modification as well as external part replacement. The gasoline tank was replaced with a sixty-gallon butane tank. These tanks were much heavier and contained a safety valve set at about 180lb pressure. The regulator was mounted on the carburetor itself. Sometimes it was called a vaporizer.

The condensed liquid fuel was ice cold. It had to be heated to make it vaporize. To start a Caterpillar Model Sixty, the motor had to run on vapor out of the top of the tank for about ten minutes. It took about this long to warm up the motor before the coolant was warm enough to heat the fuel.

But this lean mixture would burn the valves if the engine ran too long just on the vapor. So after the motor reached operating temperature, the vapor valve was turned off, and the liquid valve was opened. The regulator would vaporize the fuel before it got to the carburetor.

Converting an engine to run on butane required increased compression in addition to the carburetor modification and the addition of the regulator. For this reason, most conversions were sold most easily and accomplished most effectively when the tractor was down for an overhaul. Gasoline at that time rated 61 octane; butane rated 93 and propane was 125. The higher compression in the engine was necessary to avoid "pinging," a pre-ignition detonation of the fuel that burnt valves and could burn holes in pistons. Under normal practices, the converters put in high-rise pistons on Caterpillar Thirties, and they shaved the cylinder heads 3/4in on the Sixties. But farmers have always been tinkerers, and some of those tinkerers fancied themselves as hot-rodders too. "What if" became a question that was never asked by the people who already thought they knew the answers.

Farmers were advised to be careful. Grinding off too much from the heads meant the valves might hit the pistons. Still, farmers experimented, reasoning that if high-rise pistons were good on Model Thirties and shaved heads worked well on the Sixties, at least one farmer believed that doing both would be better. When he started up the engine, it ran for a few dozen revolutions. It made a huge racket, sounding more like a jackhammer than a tractor engine. And then it blew the crankcase studs—those holding the cylinders to the crankcase casting—out of the block.

In 1929, LPG sales had reached nearly 10 million gallons. In 1934, 56 million gallons were sold. Farmers in rice and grain country had adapted their driers to butane. In the late thirties in the Imperial Valley, dirt auto race tracks were so rough that the racers' carburetors would not stay in adjustment. Petrolane collaborated with Ensign Carburetor, which had by this time accumulated extensive experience in making LPG carburetors for dirty, dusty, high-vibration tractor conversions. The Ensign "Special" became the car to beat, and it excited local farmers with its

▲*Minneapolis-Moline advertised that its four-wheel drive system might save owners the expense of buying a crawler. The traction of its system alleviated the need for extra wheel weights. The advantage over crawlers certainly would be the ability to transport itself down the road. The full hydraulic system was available with an optional hydraulic jack that operated out of either pair of rear hydraulic hoses.*

LPG-powered performance. Then, in 1941, Minneapolis-Moline introduced the first factory-produced LPG tractors.

Testing of odorized gas began in the mid-twenties, initiated by the U.S. Bureau of Mines. The bureau found that no single odor was perfect: some people have colds, others can't smell at all, others didn't notice certain odors. Emerson Thomas, a chemical engineer with Phillips Petroleum, began odorizing Phillips' products before the U.S. regulations went into effect. Standard Oil of California tested thiophene, mixing 6.5lb per 10,000 gallons, but found it unsatisfactory. Chemists throughout the industry tested ethyl mercaptan, something the *Guinness Book of World Records* calls the smelliest substance on Earth. This is still in use, mixed at 1lb per 10,000gal. It became the U.S. standard, published in U.S. Bureau of Mines *Pamphlet* 58, in May 1932.

When war made gasoline unobtainable, LPG fell first under the rule of the War Production Board, which didn't limit production but hampered shipments due to the severe railroad tank car shortages. In 1943, the petroleum administrator for war took over LPG, and the Office of Defense Transportation moved LPG off the rails and onto the highways. By the time it all ended, hundreds of thousands of tractors throughout North America were running on LPG.

Chapter Seven

Industrial Design Comes to the Tractor

Suddenly, It's Stylish to Be a Farmer

IN MID-AUGUST 1937, ELMER MCCORMICK of Waterloo, Iowa, arrived unannounced and without an appointment at the fifth floor offices of Henry Dreyfuss Associates at 501 Madison Avenue in New York City. Dreyfuss' secretary, Rita Hart, listened to McCormick in polite amazement. Then she rushed into Dreyfuss' office and blurted out, "There's a man in a straw hat and shirt garters out there who says he is from Waterloo, Iowa and..."

"Where?" Dreyfuss asked. "Never heard of Waterloo, Iowa."

"He says he is from John Deere and he wants to see you about doing some work."

"Who," replied Henry Dreyfuss with growing interest, "is John Deere?"

While Elmer McCormick waited, Dreyfuss and Hart scrambled through the Standard & Poor's *Directory of American Corporations*. And then they opened the door and invited Mr. McCormick in to have a seat and to tell them what they could do for him and for Mr. Deere.

McCormick had traveled 1,100 miles by rail to get to New York. It had given him plenty of time to think of what he would say.

"We'd like," he began, "your help in making our tractors more salable," he concluded. And with that, he'd said his piece.

Henry Dreyfuss was born in 1904 in New York City and had graduated from the Ethical Culture School in 1922. He apprenticed for a year with Norman Bel Geddes, designing theater costumes, scenery, and sets. On his own by 1923, Dreyfuss worked for the next five years overseeing production of weekly stage shows for the Strand Theaters. By the end of 1927, he was burnt out, and he escaped to France. But he returned to New York a year later and began to solicit work as a designer. In 1929, he moved to 580 Fifth Avenue, labeled himself an industrial designer, and began to work to convince manufacturers of their need for his services.

▲*Henry Dreyfuss referred to his work on the Model A and B tractors as a "clean up." But it announced that more was to come. The first effort yielded a redesigned grille and sheet metal surrounding the steering gear and radiator, with a new operator's seat and foot platform. Within a couple of years, Dreyfuss and his associates would be involved in complete tractor design beginning at the pre-planning stages.*

▶*Initially, Deere's request to industrial designer Henry Dreyfuss was for help in making the tractors "more salable." The economy had finally turned around after the Depression and advertising and sales people wanted something they could boast was "new and improved" to get the farm family visit to the local agent for a look. These are both 1938 Model BWHs.*

Through the next several years, he devised and formalized his philosophy into what he referred to as a five-point formula. It was based on emphasizing an object's function, that its form should result from its intended use. He paid particular attention to such considerations as the utility and safety of the object, its ease of maintenance, its cost to produce, its sales appeal and, last but not least, its appearance.

The motto, really a treatise, in the office lobby explained the practical application of Dreyfuss' philosophy.

"We bear in mind," it said, "that the object being worked on is going to be ridden in, sat upon, looked at, talked to, activated, operated or in some other way used by the people individually or en masse. When the point of contact between the product and the people becomes a point of friction, then the industrial designer has failed. On the other hand, if people are made safer, more comfortable, more eager to purchase, more efficient—or just plain happier—by contact with the product, then the designer has succeeded."

With that message in front of him, McCormick knew he had come to the right place. After a night in the Waldorf Astoria, McCormick joined Dreyfuss, and they took the morning train headed back west to Waterloo.

What Dreyfuss accomplished has been characterized as merely "a clean up." Perhaps this was the perspective from the designers who would participate in the many great changes to come. But to the farmer, the appearance and the function were so much improved that a word was coined to refer to the effect. Henceforth, tractors—whether "cleaned up" or changed greatly by Henry Dreyfuss or his colleagues, Raymond

JOHN DEERE
JOHN DEERE

JOHN DEERE

JOHN DEERE

SILVER KING

▸▸ Dreyfuss' first sketches for Deere and Company tractors were dated August 1937, shortly after his first meeting. The tractors he drew were Model Bs that incorporated the steering wheel shafts and gear and the radiator behind a streamlined, powerful-looking steel housing. There are dozens of differences between the two machines, both sold in 1938, both Model Bs.

◂ The 1936 Silver King R72 ran on 10.00x24.0in rear tires and a single 6.00x16 front. It measured 67in tall, 78in wide, and 128in long overall, on a 70in wheelbase. It weighed only 2,200lb. It was offered on steel wheels or low-pressure inflatable rubber and was tested both ways at the University of Nebraska.

Loewy or Walter Dorwin Teague—were forever known as "styled" tractors. Those not bearing the industrial designers' improvements remained "unstyled."

It was a curious word choice. Industrial designers balk at being called "stylists." And the tractors received much more than mere appearance improvements. There were, even from the start, fundamental design changes, and subsequent tractors received engineering changes as part of the Dreyfuss industrial design process for Deere & Co. This was quite similar to work done for International Harvester by Raymond Loewy. But the manufacturers already had engineers and designers on the payroll and some method had to be designated to explain which of the tractors were new and which were old to the board of directors, the branch salesmen, and the farmers. The vague word "styled" did that quite simply.

Before the end of August 1937, Henry Dreyfuss and Associates had prepared more than a half-dozen design studies for new

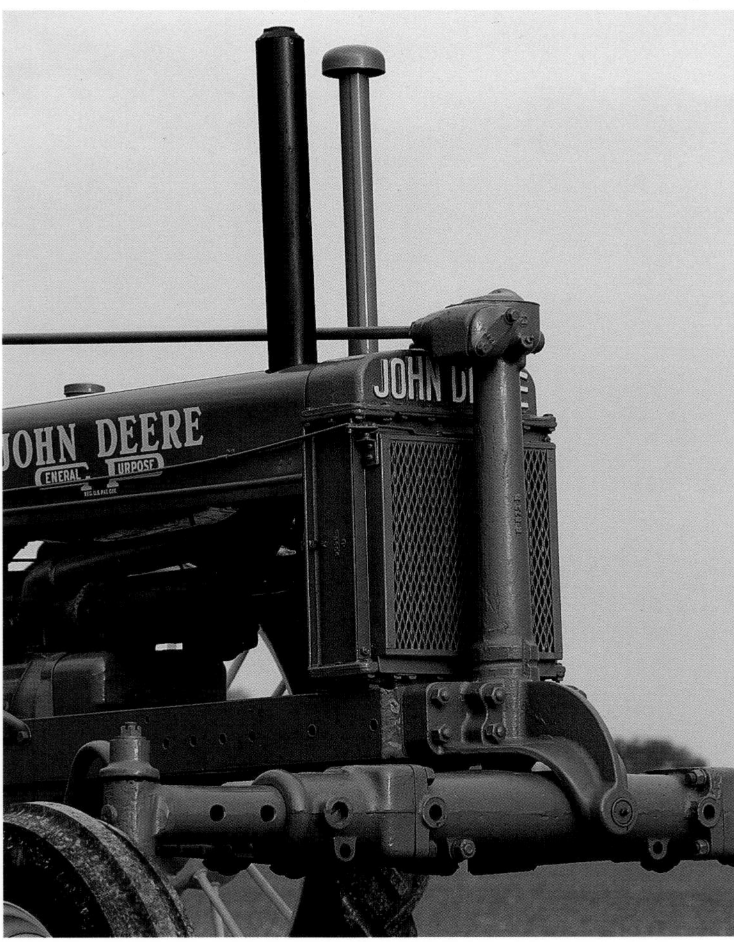

▴ Deere & Co. knew its customers and even with its confidence in Dreyfuss' work, Deere hedged its bets. It recognized that as desirable as "new and improved" was to some people, to others, this was all too new. The old didn't need improvement anyway. For several years, Deere continued to sell unstyled machines right alongside the styled ones.

1937
C K BRECHEISEN
SILVER KING

sheet metal for Deere's Model A and B. A combination of elements from several of the studies became the landmark styled John Deere tractor. These new lines enclosed the steering column and radiator behind a strong-looking grille. But the improvements also affected function, because the narrower radiator cowling and gas tank covering improved visibility forward and down. The instrument panel was redesigned and better organized for the farmer's readability while bouncing through the fields. The back end of the tractor received attention too, as the Dreyfuss designers "cleaned up" its appearance, at the same time making it easier to recognize the different functions of the various fittings.

The tractor seat was an object of serious concern to Dreyfuss and his designers. Farmers sat behind a vertical wheel almost in front of their faces. But with the small rear wheels common in the late twenties and early thirties, every bump over a plowed field was magnified; standing at least allowed the legs to absorb the shock.

So the steering wheel was, logically, set up high. When the operators stood, they could lean against it, putting their hand right on top of it. What was worse, however, was that even with the tractor at rest, the seat didn't fit the average human body.

Dreyfuss once asked Deere & Co. management how they de-

▲*The 1936 Model R72 used a Hercules type IXB in-line four-cylinder engine of 3.25x4.0in bore and stroke. A Fairbanks-Morse RV4 magneto and a Zenith 1.5in carburetor were standard. At 1,400rpm, the engine produced a maximum of 19.7 belt pulley horsepower and 16.4hp on the drawbar. The four-speed transmission offered 25mph top speed on rubber tires.*

◂*In the foreground, the 1936 Silver King Model R72 faces off against the 1940 Model 41. The differences are large despite the styling similarities. Both were manufactured by Fate-Root-Heath Co., of Plymouth, Ohio. Both were restored and are owned by Paul Brecheisen of Helena, Ohio.*

▲*The 1936, shown here, used the Hercules. Later models used a Continental Red Seal type F162 four-cylinder with a Marvel-Schebler carburetor and a Bosch magneto connected to Delco electrics. Top speed was nearly 30mph. Fate-Root-Heath continued to produce the Silver King until 1956.*

MASSEY-
HARRIS
Challenger
FRONT
31686F
REAR
31686F

The in-line four-cylinder engine had 3.875x5.25in bore and stroke. At 1,200rpm, the tractor produced 16.3 drawbar and a maximum of 27.2 belt pulley horsepower. It used a Kingston 1.25in carburetor and a Bosch U4 magneto. The tractor weighed about 4,300lb on rubber tires. This 1937 model was restored and is owned by Wes Stoelk of Westside, Iowa.

The Challenger was introduced in 1936 as Toronto, Ontario-based Massey-Harris' first row-crop tractor. It was offered on steel or rubber and production ended at the end of 1938. The curved boiler plate sheet beneath the engine served not only as the bottom engine and transmission case but also as the structural frame for the tractor.

signed their early seat. Dreyfuss had developed his Human Forms, a thorough collection of measurements and dimensions for a fictional Joe and Josephine. Those male and female "models" allowed Dreyfuss to design virtually any action or apparatus to fit any size person. The Deere tractor seat did not fit *any* Joe or Josephine.

Elmer McCormick told Dreyfuss that they used Pete. Deere managers looked around the factory one day to find the fellow with the biggest behind, and they had him sit in plaster. That became the seat size.

Styled Model A and B tractors were introduced to the public for the 1938 season. While these were at first viewed with caution by the same farmers who had vilified the sissies on rubber tires, they were quickly taken up by the branch salesmen who, at last, had something dramatically "new and improved" to sell. When the advertising brochures and service manuals were produced for the new-looking Model A and B, Deere pronounced them "Tomorrow's tractor today."

The risk of selling yesterday's tractor today forced International Harvester, Massey-Harris, Ford, Cockshutt, Oliver, Minneapolis-Moline, Allis-Chalmers, J. I. Case, and many of the independents to jump into the Streamline Age bandwagon with their checkbooks open. Raymond Loewy was hired to do not only IHC's tractors but also its showrooms and even a new, bolder corporate logo. His creation resembled a front view of a row-

▲*The International Harvester Company (IHC) built its own engines, this one being an in-line four-cylinder of 4.25x5.0in bore and stroke. Running at 1,150rpm, the engine produced a maximum 24.8hp on the drawbar and 30.3 belt pulley horsepower. IHC made their own magnetos; this one was the E4A model. The Zenith K5 carburetor was standard equipment.*

▸*The F-30 was introduced on steel but, as all manufacturers adopted rubber, the choice was left to the purchaser. Ray Pollock of Vail, Iowa, acquired this tractor in 1948 and, until his recent retirement from active farming, used it every day year round. In more than forty-five years of use, his most major repair was to grind the valves on two separate occasions.*

crop tractor with an operator in place.

Industrial design arrived at different times and in different degrees at other manufacturers. In 1928, brothers Joseph, Robert, and Ray Graham acquired the Paige automobile company and began producing striking, sleek automobiles. A decade later, they were manufacturing a general purpose tractor that was sold through Sears Catalog and was as stylish, attractive, and practical as any of their cars.

In some cases, industrial design changed the colors of tractors. In 1938, all of the green tractors carried over from the Wallis designs became red and wrapped in louvered, streamlined sheet metal as part of the Massey-Harris line. Minneapolis-Mo-

FARMALL

▲*International introduced the original Farmall model for sale in 1924, at $950. By late 1931, when the Farmall-30 was introduced, prices had increased only to $1,110. For the model year 1937 and 1938, the price on inflatable rubber tires was $1,225. IHC sold F-30s into 1940, using up inventory on hand after engine production ceased in late 1939. This is the 1938 model.*

▸*When Massey-Harris entered the age of "styled" tractors, no company made a more dramatic change in appearance between its 1937 models such as the Challenger and the streamlined Super Twin-Power 101s. The multitude of louvers was a visual cue taken from automobile designs of the late thirties. But the louvers did not offer enough airflow to cool the hard-working engine. Later Massey-Harris tractors had open sides.*

◂*In 1920, farms in the United States operated on 25 million horses and mules and 200,000 tractors. It took a war in Europe and then a much different price war back home to change those proportions. The post-war Depression slowed down the conversion through the early thirties. But the introduction of cost-effective, powerful tractors such as the Farmall F-30 turned the tables. By 1940, the horse population was down to about 14 million while nearly 1.6 million tractors now worked the fields. Nearly 250,000 tractors were manufactured in 1938 alone.*

line evolved from gray with red trim to prairie gold. On Friday, September 23, 1938, it hosted 12,000 guests at its Farm Equipment Style Show at the Minneapolis Auditorium to show off its stunning new Model U-DLX Comfortractor, one piece of the fall collection of new Visionlined tractors. These machines looked more modern than some automobiles available at the time and, in the case of the U-DLX, they were even meant to replace them. In 1957, Cockshutt introduced its aggressive, purposeful-looking 500-series in two-tone paint schemes, designed by Raymond Loewy's group. These wider, more massive tractors replaced the art-deco stylish delicacy of the nearly all-red 1947 Model 30 that had been designed by architectural designer Charlie Brooks.

Industrial designers are interdisciplinary. Although Norman Bel Geddes, Walter Dorwin Teague, and Raymond Loewy all came from advertising, they and Henry Dreyfuss quickly under-

MASSEY-HARRIS
MASSEY HARRIS

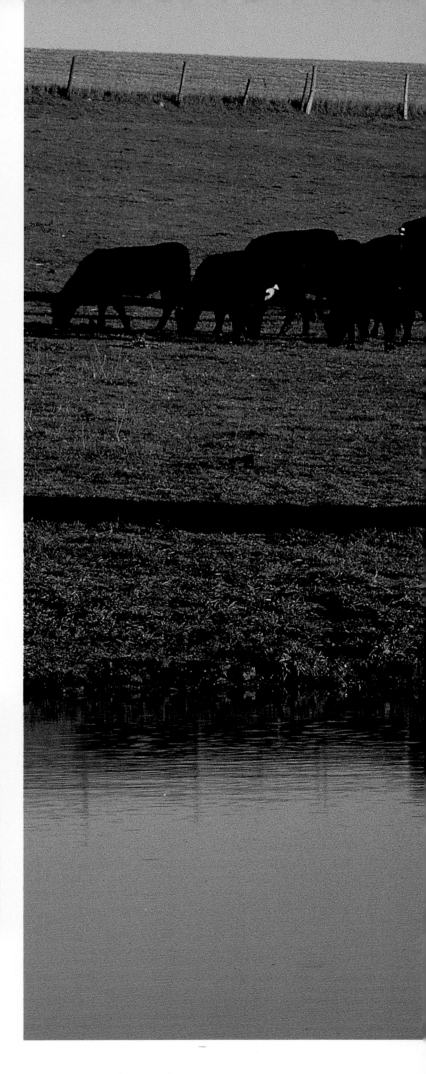

The startling styling wasn't the only new development to come out of the Massey-Harris design department. A complete change in color sparked up the appearance of Massey-Harris tractors on the fields of North America. As the continent moved out of the Depression, advertising and sales managers sought to make the tractors more eye-catching even as the engineers worked to make the machines more efficient.

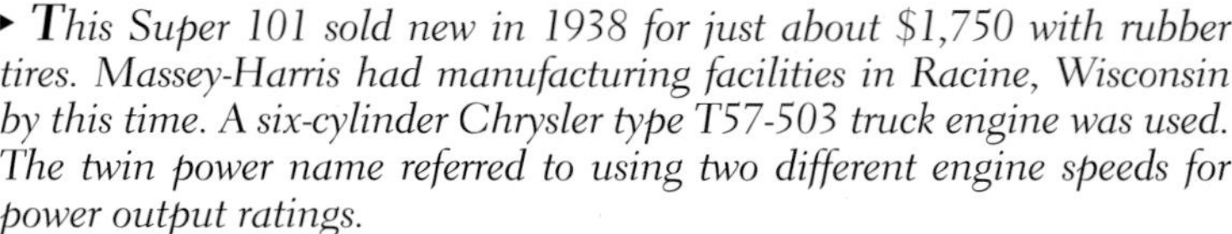

This Super 101 sold new in 1938 for just about $1,750 with rubber tires. Massey-Harris had manufacturing facilities in Racine, Wisconsin by this time. A six-cylinder Chrysler type T57-503 truck engine was used. The twin power name referred to using two different engine speeds for power output ratings.

The engine measured 3.125x4.375in bore and stroke. Its maximum drawbar power was 31.5hp at 1,500rpm while its peak belt pulley performance was 40.7hp at 1,800rpm, hence the Twin-Power name. A Marvel-Schebler 1in carburetor and an AutoLite electrical system with starter were standard. This machine was restored and is owned by Wes Stoelk of Westside, Iowa.

MASSEY-
HARRIS

◂ *One of the most controversial products of styling was the Comfortractor. Minneapolis-Moline fitted the Model U not only with the enclosed, heated three-plus seat cabin but also with a road gear capable of 40mph. With the Model U-DLX, Minneapolis-Moline hoped farmers would not need an automobile. On Sunday morning, simply hose off the tractor and drive the family to church. Farmers had a built-in radio to keep them company during field work. The side windows rolled down and windshield wipers swept away the rain.*

▴ *The striking 1938 U-DLX was not an unqualified success. Mechanically, it was a reliable tractor. But farmers, accustomed to modesty and humility, looked on it as excessive. Even the justifiable pride in ownership that some owners felt about their Comfortractors put others off. Somehow, it seemed nobler to freeze in the winter or soak in the rain. In the end, barely 125 were sold. It would be years before any other manufacturer would introduce fully-enclosed, heated cabs.*

stood that they needed to be fluent with the languages and techniques of engineering, mechanics, manufacturing, sales, marketing, and metallurgy to make their work most effective.

As Jeffrey Meikle observed in an essay in the 1993 book, *Industrial Design: Reflection Of A Century*, "Dramatic evidence of the economic benefit of designing for mass production came in 1927, when Henry Ford abandoned production of his beloved Model T, a car that transformed American life, and spent $18 million on the newly designed Model A. This 'most expensive art lesson in history,' as someone called it, offered proof to manufacturers that visual appearance had become critically important in marketing ordinary consumer goods. As the business recession of the late twenties expanded into fully fledged economic depression, manufacturers turned to product redesign, at first as a tool for overcoming competition in their own industries, but later as a panacea for restoring the nation's economic health."

Like the electric self-starter replacing the crank, industrial design was seen first by the manufacturers as an easier way to restart farmers' interests in buying new machines. Exactly like the electric self-starter, it became the means for farmers to understand how much easier the tractor was to use, and then to imagine how much more it could do for them.

STANDARD 88
OLIVER
88

▲*Oliver used its own in-line six-cylinder engine with 3.5x4.0in bore and stroke. At 1,600rpm, the engine produced 29.1 drawbar horsepower and a maximum of 41.0 belt pulley horsepower. The tractors offered either a four-speed forward/four-speed reverse transmission, or one with six speeds forward. Front tires were 6.00x16 while rears were 14x26.*

◂*Morning sun melted off the hard frost and created a haze in the field behind the late Tiny Blom's 1947 Model 88 Standard. Oliver's designers produced some of the most attractive tractors with the cleanest lines of any of the makes during the era of streamlining and styling. The Model 88 was introduced in late 1947 and remained in production until 1954.*

▲*The Standard measured 74in high, 72in wide, and 132in overall. Two transmissions were offered. One provided four speeds forward and four reverse. The other had six speed forward and two in reverse. Top road speed in sixth gear was 11.8mph. Front tires were 6.00x16 while rears were either 13x26 or 14x26.*

▶*The Standard 88 sold new for $2,603 in gasoline, $3,456 in diesel. Oliver referred to their sheet-metal enclosed streamlined tractors as the "Fleetline Series." Oliver discovered as Massey-Harris had found, that fully enclosed engines suffered from insufficient air flow for cooling. Later models had open sides.*

STANDARD
88

▾*Offset seating and steering kept body width to a minimum on the Model UTC high clearance tractor. Minneapolis-Moline used its own in-line four-cylinder engine with bore and stroke of 4.25x5.0in for total capacity of 283ci. At 1,300rpm, it recorded a maximum of 33.5hp off the drawbar and 37.2hp on the belt pulley. The tractor weighed about 5,750lb.*

▸*The high-clearance model allowed 24in below the drawbar. The tractor stood 105in tall to the top of the exhaust, 81in wide, 134in long overall, and had an 80in wheelbase. Front tires were 7.50x18 while the rears were 14.9x38. Most high ground clearance tractors were destined for work in cotton and sugar cane applications in the southern states and Hawaii.*

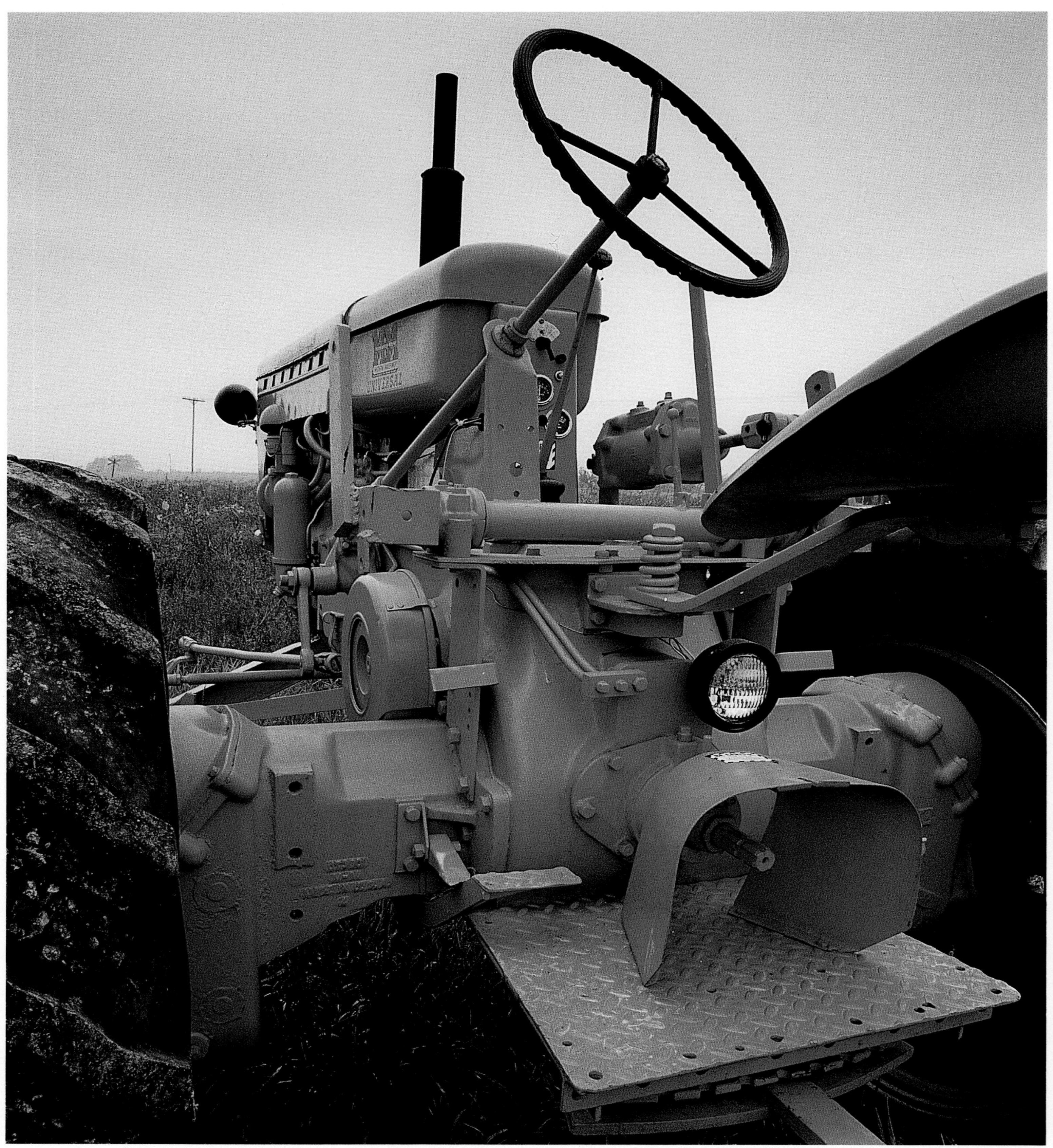

▸*Minneapolis-Moline used the term "Visionlined" to describe what Deere & Co. called styled. These new harvest gold tractors were introduced to thousands of customers in a "Style" show in the Minneapolis Auditorium in 1938 as direct competition with Deere, Massey-Harris, and International Harvester. This is the 1946 Model UTC.*

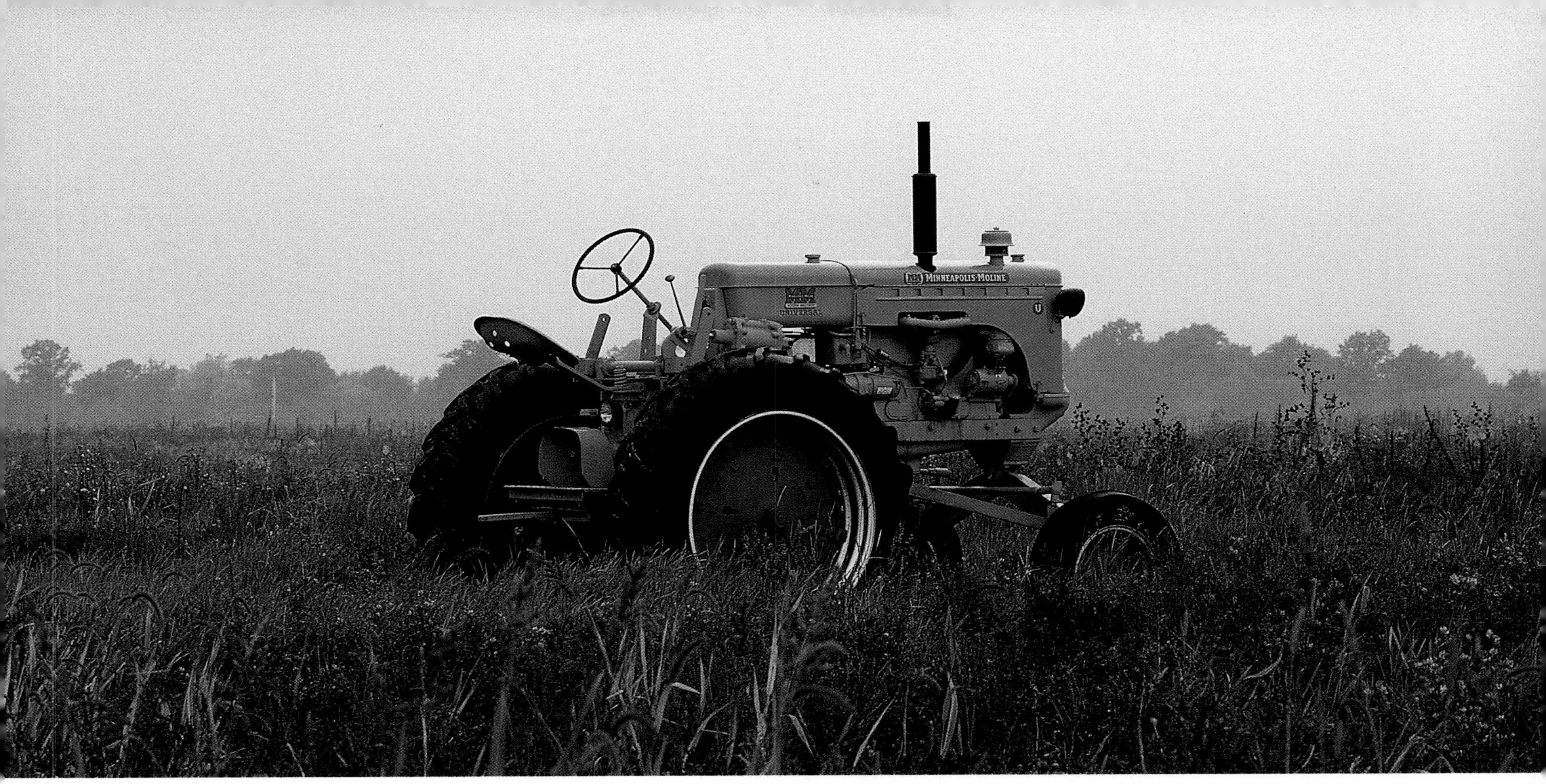
MINNEAPOLIS-MOLINE

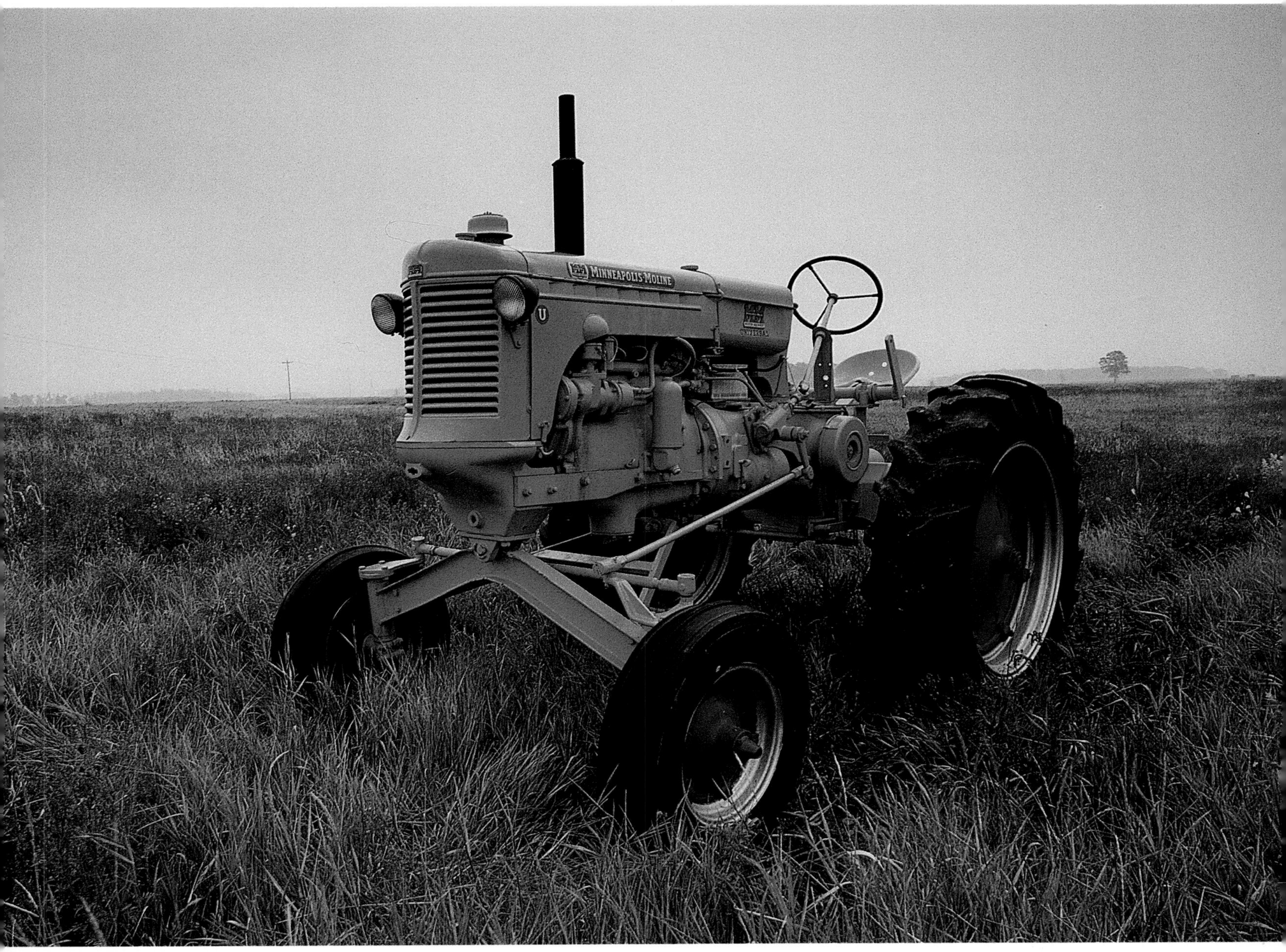
MINNEAPOLIS-MOLINE

CASE

CASE
VAC
CASE
CASE

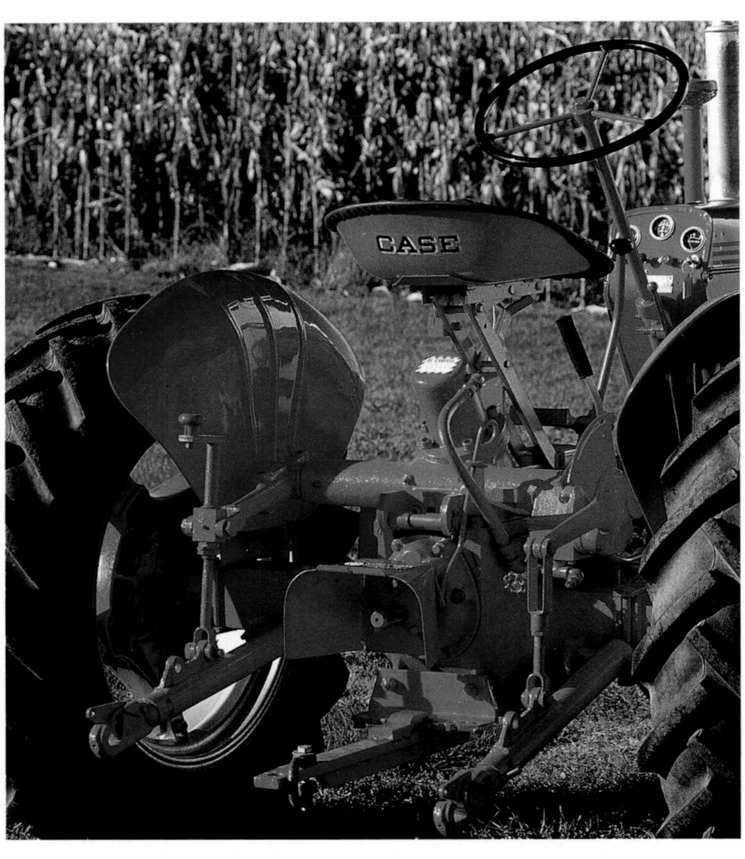

◂◂ *Case introduced its Model VAC tractors in 1942 and sold them into the early fifties. Rear tread width was adjustable from 48–88in. The 1949 wide-front has the three-point Eagle-Hitch system. These two tractors were restored and are owned by Raynard Schmidt of Vail, Iowa.*

▸ *The Case engine measured 3.25x3.75in bore and stroke and produced 12.5 drawbar and a maximum 17.0 belt pulley horsepower at 1,425rpm during its University of Nebraska tests. A Marvel-Schebler carburetor and AutoLite electrics were standard equipment. The wide-front version weighed slightly more than 3,200lb. Front tires were 6.00x12 on the 1948 single, 5.00x15 on the wide and rears were 11x28 on the wide, 10x28 on the single.*

◂ *The crank screw on the left hitch arm was used to adjust the arms for implement depth or to level them for some harvesting purposes. The top link was removed here because the owner uses the wide-front VAC to tow wagons during corn harvest. Other implements such as cultivators were attached by lever linkage ahead of the rear tires.*

▾ *The 1949 wide-front Model VAC was only one of a variety of VA-tractor configurations that J.I. Case offered. An industrial model VAI was introduced with the entire series in 1942. In 1943, Case offered the first orchard tractors, the VAO, with much of the engine, rear tires, and operators' position enclosed in sheet metal. A single-front and a dual-front row crop model were available and in 1948, a VAH high-clearance model was introduced. For 1952, the VAS provided high-clearance with an offset operators position, the better to cultivate single rows of tomatoes, tobacco, and cotton.*

CASE
VAC

▲*The Model R was introduced in 1939 and in 1940 it was offered with a fitted cab after the style of the Model U-DLX Comfortractor. A number of high-clearance versions of these enclosed tractors were modified with baskets alongside the engine and over the front wheels; these were produced for the U.S. Post Office for use as rural mail carriers.*

▸*Minneapolis-Moline was the first company to bring cabs to a wide audience. Both the U-DLX and the RT used a rear door, which obviously precluded any possibility of utilizing the power-take-off shaft. The tractor measured 83in tall to the top of the rear light, 79in wide, and only 119in long overall. Front tires were Firestone 4.0x15 while rears were 9.0x36.*

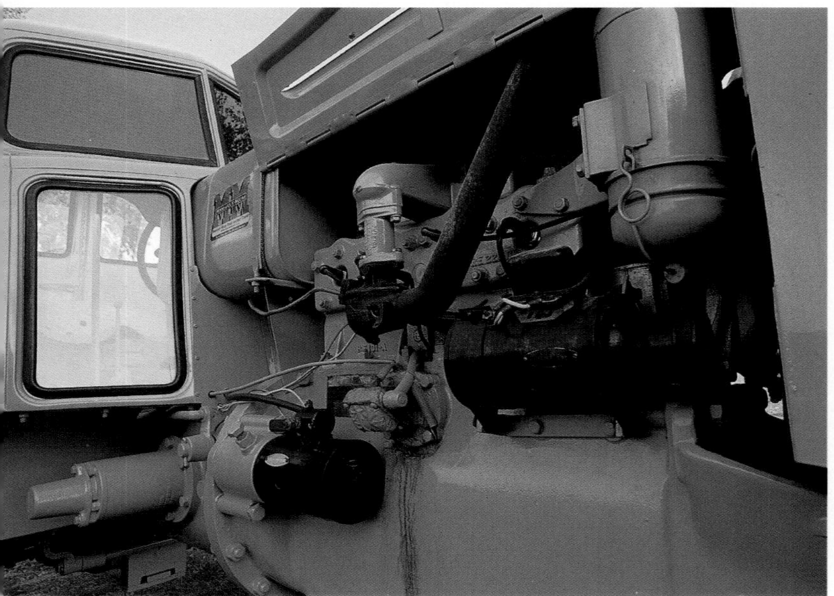

▲*Minneapolis-Moline's in-line four-cylinder 3.625x4.0in engine had a total capacity of 165ci. At 1,500rpm, 18.3hp on the drawbar and 25.9hp on the belt pulley were achieved. Top speed of the non-postal service-modified Rs was 13.2mph. The R sold for $1,500 with cab. This example was restored and is owned by Walter and Bruce Keller of Kaukauna, Wisconsin.*

▲*The cab interior of the 1951 RT was spartan compared to the U-DLX. Without radio, heater, rear-view mirror, or fold-down seat for a passenger, farmers were more inclined to look at the RT as a proper machine. The seat in the R swiveled for operator ease in entry and exit. The cab itself was 42in from windshield to door, 36in wide, and 55in tall.*

MM
MINNEAPOLIS-MOLINE

▲Rodney Ott's well-used 1954 Super 88 Standard worked nearly every day of its life tending his farm near Hilbert, Wisconsin. As the successor to the Oliver 88, one distinctive visible change was that the side panels around the engine were opened for better air circulation. Oliver offered single and narrow row-crop front axles as well as both adjustable and fixed tread wide fronts.

▸The Super 88 sold for around $3,800 when it was introduced in 1954. The Oliver 256ci six-cylinder engine had bore and stroke of 3.75x4.0in. During its Nebraska tests, it produced 36.8 hp on the drawbar and a maximum of 49.6hp on the belt pulley. The Super 88 would reach 11.75mph in 6th gear at 1,600rpm. It weighed 5,513lb with fuel and operator.

▸*Just as nearly all the other makers had discovered, fully enclosed side panels, even if fully louvered, trapped too much heat. The Model 333 used Massey's four-cylinder 3.69x4.875in engine. It yielded 29.7hp at the drawbar and a maximum of 39.8hp on the belt pulley at 1,500rpm.*

▾*The Model 333 featured a ten-speed forward/two-speed reverse transmission, offering a speed range from 1.5 to 14mph. Row-crop versions ran on 5.50x16in front tires and 12.0x28in rears. The late fifties marked the end of streamlined styling as makers moved toward more massive, aggressive appearances to reflect the increase in power that was coming from the engineers. Wes Stoelk and his son Scott of Westside, Iowa, restored and own this 1956 tractor.*

▲*As good as this hitch was, it was about to get better. Massey's Depth-O-Matic hydraulics would quickly become the legendary Ferguson three-point hitch. Power steering was also available on the Model 333. The 333 could also be had in standard and high-clearance models. The tractor was sold only in 1956 and 1957 and retailed for $2,838 for this gasoline row-crop version.*

◂*In 1953, the sun set on one Canadian manufacturing name and rose on a more international blend. Massey-Harris added the name of Harry Ferguson when it merged with the Irish inventor of the three-point hitch. New tractors under Ferguson's influence didn't appear until 1959, however.*

Chapter Eight

Ford, Ferguson and the Three-Point Hitch

THE HANDSHAKE HEARD 'ROUND THE WORLD

"WHAT A WASTE IT IS," HENRY FORD ONCE remarked, "for a human being to spend hours and days behind a slow moving team of horses." He gained that perspective from practical experience. It cleared his vision. "The farmer must either take up power or go out of business," he judged. "Power farming is simply taking the burden from flesh and blood and putting it on steel."

In his 1926 book, *My Life and Work*, he reflected, "The automobile is designed to carry; the tractor is designed to pull. The public was more interested in being carried than in being pulled; the horseless carriage made a greater appeal to the imagination." So, with regret, he put aside development of tractors to work on automobiles for a while. But he waited only until the number of automobiles in the world sparked the demand for better, cheaper, lighter, and more manageable tractors.

For Ford, the future of the farm tractor pulled sharply away from the past. The large, heavy steam tractors grew out of the theory that weight meant power. Yet, if tractors were to pull rather than carry, excess weight detracted from the capacity to pull. Ford reasoned that his tractor had to be light yet strong, simple to operate, and yet cheap to buy and maintain. Cost was important. Anyone who wanted a tractor should be able to get one. Having and using it with ease was a key to his greater goal of making food and clothing more affordable as well.

It seems, in retrospect, that Ford thought and spoke in eloquent sound bites; it is close to true. He was one of North America's most public industrialists. Born in 1863, he was the second generation Ford in North America born onto farmland outside Dearborn, Michigan. Grandfather John emigrated from his own small farm near Cork, Ireland, in 1847, to settle near relatives in Michigan. He bought 80 acres for $350. Henry's father, William, added land and expected his son, Henry, to follow the family tradition. But to Henry, farming was drudgery. He preferred to tinker with machines. In 1896, his first machine ran, and by 1903, his motor company had begun. Ford started his first serious tractor experiments late in 1905. He established a satellite "tractor works" just three blocks from his main plant. He worked through several tractor attempts. Then in 1907, a prototype using the Model B engine was sent to his nearby Fair Lane farm for testing. Two more prototypes emerged and were tested through the fall and winter. In 1910, Ford applied for several patents even though tractor manufacture had taken a back seat to the automobile. His board of directors was unimpressed. The board disapproved of his plans to manufacture tractors at the new Highland Park plant. So in 1915, he left his own company over these disputes, and incorporated his new tractor company, Henry Ford & Son, in July 1917. (The Ford name was registered by Minneapolis businessman Baer Ewing, who produced a tractor, the Ford Model B, hoping to capitalize on the confusion. See chapter three.)

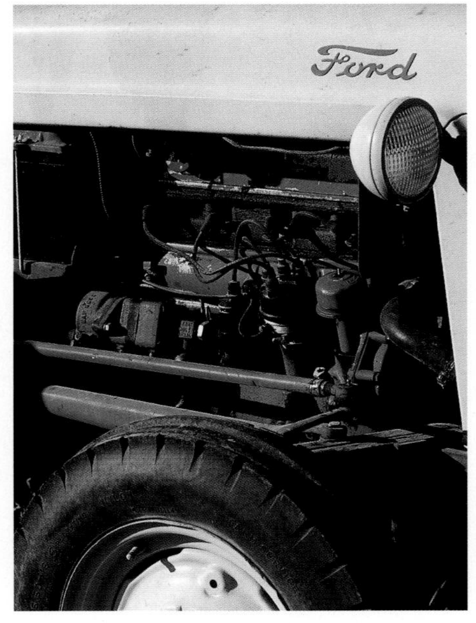

▲*With 3.44x3.6in bore and stroke, the new NAA engine provided a peak 20.2 drawbar horsepower at 1,750rpm and a maximum of 30.2hp at 2,000rpm on the belt pulley. Even with a twenty percent increase in power, fuel economy remained 11.2 horsepower hours per gallon.*

▸*By the time Henry Ford celebrated his fiftieth year in business during 1953, peace and tranquillity had nearly returned to his life and his business. The break up with Ferguson was nearly resolved, and his Golden Jubilee was a new, improved machine. A 4in longer wheelbase, 5in longer overall, and 100lb heavier, it also boasted a new 134ci overhead valve engine.*

Ford collected samples of nearly every competitors' tractors. He tested them on his farm, then gathered them at the new Dearborn plant for his staff to examine. Because efficient manufacture was as important to Ford as product affordability, the tractor was designed in three units: a transmission housing contained the gearbox, differential, and the worm and worm wheel drive to the rear axle; the engine included flywheel and clutch assemblies; and the front end included mounts for the steering assembly and axle. Ford intended the tractor parts to be strong enough to support the entire ma-

Ford

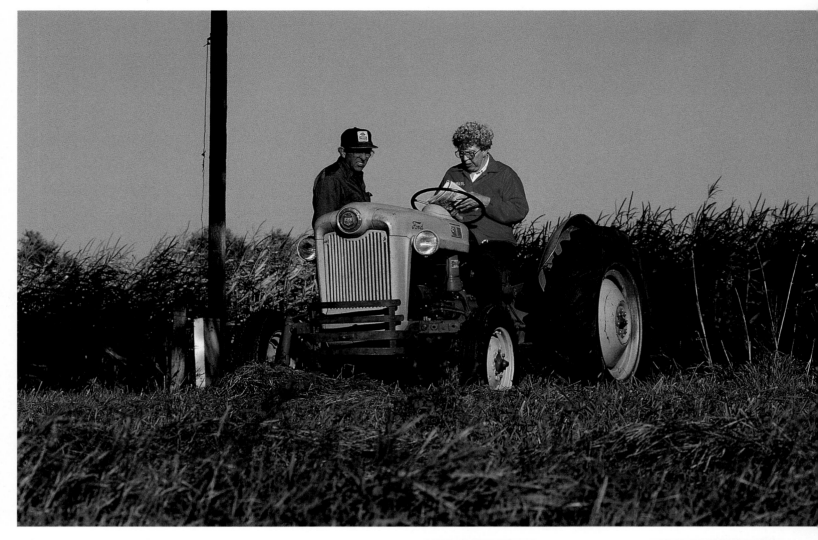

▲*Harriet Fossum sets off to work while husband Palmer looks on. Much like what occurred at thousands of other farms, Harriet learned to operate a tractor when she was ten, taught by her father. She operated a grain binder and a bale loader. When Palmer went off to the Korean War, Harriet—like millions of soldier's wives before her—joined the work force. She worked nights as a nurse while, all around her, women kept farms operating and food on the tables throughout the U.S. and Canada.*

▸*It's simple if you know what it means. Drawbar horsepower peaked at 1,750rpm yet the engine could handle belt loads up to 2,000rpm. The needle indicated ground speeds in each gear at an indicated engine speed. Top speed in fourth gear was quoted by Ford to be about 11.5mph, at roughly 1,750rpm.*

chine without needing a separate frame. In his factory, all these units were designed to be run on rails to a central point for final assembly. He had used vanadium steel in the Model T, but chrome carbon steel was introduced for the tractors.

The first production run of fifty went back to Fair Lane farm for testing. Word leaked out. Stories appeared in magazines and newspapers. The world knew Ford's car; now it learned that his tractor was coming.

World War I had begun in Europe. The Germans were sinking a ship a day. England was losing its farmers and able-bodied draft animals and its food. With such losses, the British government sought help to encourage farm tractor production in the United Kingdom. Then on April 6, 1916, the United States entered the war. Ford sent Charles Sorensen, his assistant, to England with a carload of parts, patterns, and implements. He was to find a suitable factory, but at the end of June, the Germans bombed London's Fleet Street financial district. All the possible tractor plants were rushed into war plane manufacture; the tractors had to come from the United States.

Cables went to Ford. The British government ordered a minimum of 5,000 Fordsons at cost-plus-$50, about $700 each. First delivery was to be within sixty days! Sorensen returned home. The Dearborn plant was not yet ready, and the facility at Highland Park was working at capacity on war materiel. Later, limits in available shipping space slowed delivery. But somehow, Ford found a way. By early December, Fordsons began to arrive in England. A total of 7,000 were there by the spring of 1917.

Britain had lost 350,000 farm hands by the time the Fordsons arrived. The food situation was desperate, and the government

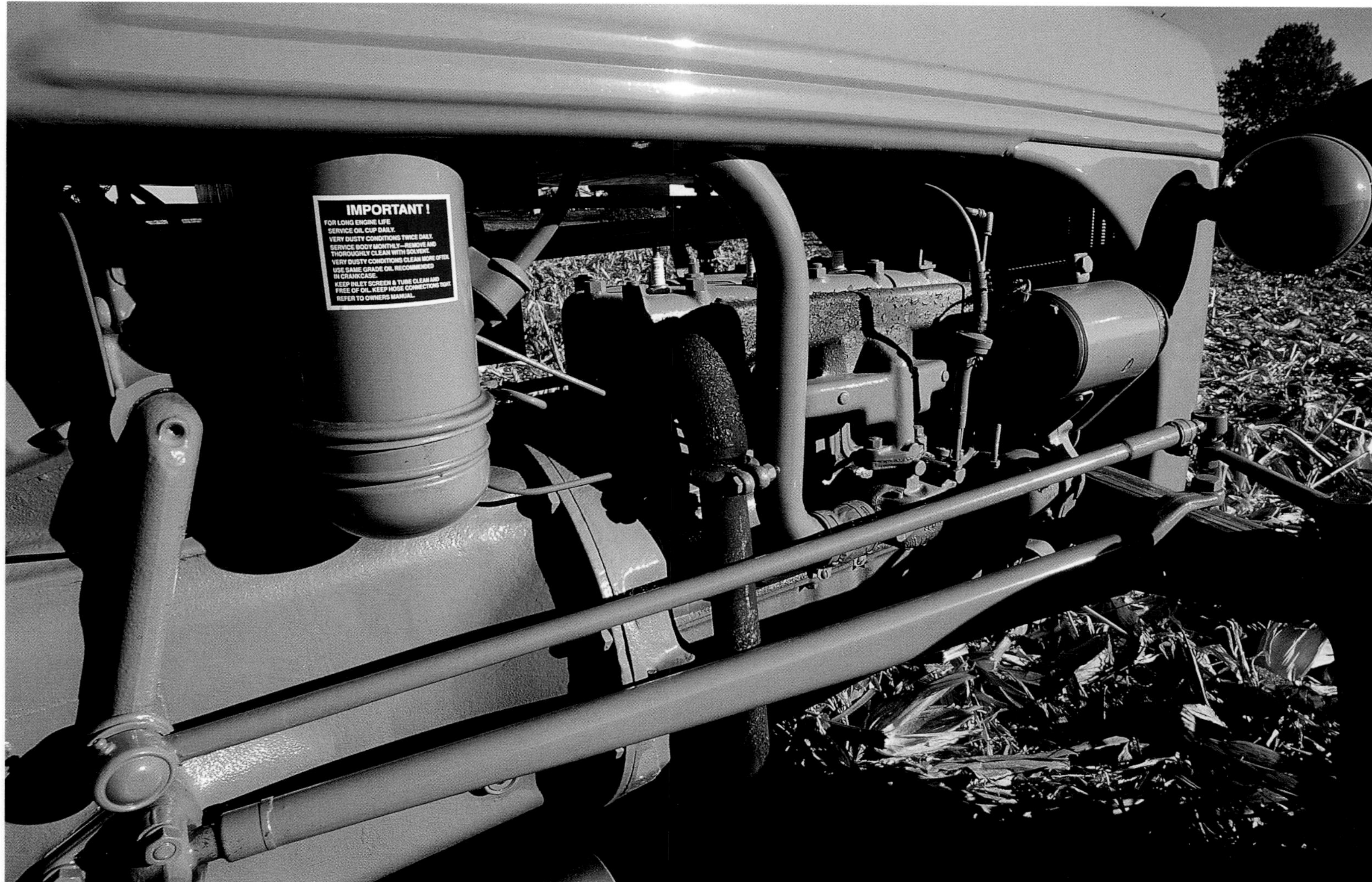

▲The nomenclature of the Ford-Ferguson tractors is fairly common knowledge: the 9, 2, and 8 refer to 1939, 1942, and 1948 as introduction years for the series. The 2N designation came as a corporate decision regarding governmental restrictions on raw materials at the beginning of World War II. Only by introducing a new model could certain supplies be made available or could prices be increased. (Deere & Co. did something similar with their Model G and GM.) This is the 1942 Model 2N.

asked farmers to cultivate an additional 500,000 acres in 1917.

In Ireland, where most of this new land was to be opened up, Harry Ferguson, an aviator and auto racer, had already taken the tractor into his heart and his business. He had begun selling the Overtime, the London-built Waterloo Boy.

Ferguson, the fourth child of James Ferguson, was born in 1884, and raised on the family's 100-acre farm, 16mi south of Belfast. As with Ford, Ferguson did his farm chores, but anything mechanical easily lured him away from the farm. He was saved when his oldest brother, Joe, hired him to apprentice at his automobile workshop in Belfast.

Ferguson found himself. Machines became his passion. He even built his own airplane. He succeeded in every endeavor through salesmanship and showmanship. By the time the war in Europe approached the United Kingdom, he was in business for himself, and the need for food married Ferguson's work with his enthusiasm for machines. He jumped into tractor demonstrations with his Overtime. As a result of his successes, the Irish government approached him. To improve tractor performance nationwide, they asked him to visit farmers to perform educational shows. While doing these shows, Ferguson saw mostly tractors imported from the United States. While he found many of these cumbersome to use, what concerned him was the inefficiency and danger in the single-point plow hitch.

With Ireland's soil, the risk of hanging up the plow on hidden rocks was great. Horses simply stopped moving. Tractors with a spinning flywheel tended to keep going. Often that motion simply wound the tractor around the final drive gear and brought the nose up. If the operator didn't quickly put in the clutch, the tractor would flip over. It took quick reactions to release the clutch. Ferguson saw farmers with slower reactions missing arms or legs when their tractors flipped. He met the widows of those not so fortunate as that.

Even if the impact did not flip the tractor, the plow was usually damaged after impact. Farmers were advised to use wooden shear pins to attach the plows, but turning a field for the first time could exhaust a large supply of pins. Another drawback Ferguson witnessed was that while using implements designed for horse-drawn farming, tractor farmers often did not get satisfactory results. Plows had their own wheels, a vast improvement over earlier versions that the farmers not only had to steer but also carry! These wheels also served to set furrow depth. But over uneven soil, with the drawbar rising and falling as the tractor moved along, the furrow height either needed constant adjustment or simply ended up sloppy and uneven.

Harry Ferguson came to understand the tractor makers' motivation for great weight. It not only kept traction to the drive wheels, but it held down the plow. Nevertheless, he was con-

▸*Harry Ferguson produced not only hitches but a full range of plows to work off them. That was the single most significant difference between him and handshake-partner Henry Ford. Ford never saw the need for or any advantage in producing specific Ford-built implements coupled to his tractors. Ford missed income possibilities and received the blame when others implements failed to perform well on his tractors. Here, a Ferguson quarter-turn 16in bottom plow waits for work to begin.*

vinced there was a better way.

Back in Dearborn, Henry Ford & Son tractor company was busy. Within three months of completing the British shipment, Ford had delivered more than 5,000 of the backlog of some 13,000 North American orders. By April 1918, daily production was sixty-four. In July, 131 Fordsons rolled out of the Dearborn plant every day.

It didn't take much time to uncover the Fordson's shortcomings. The early design set the worm and worm gear right below

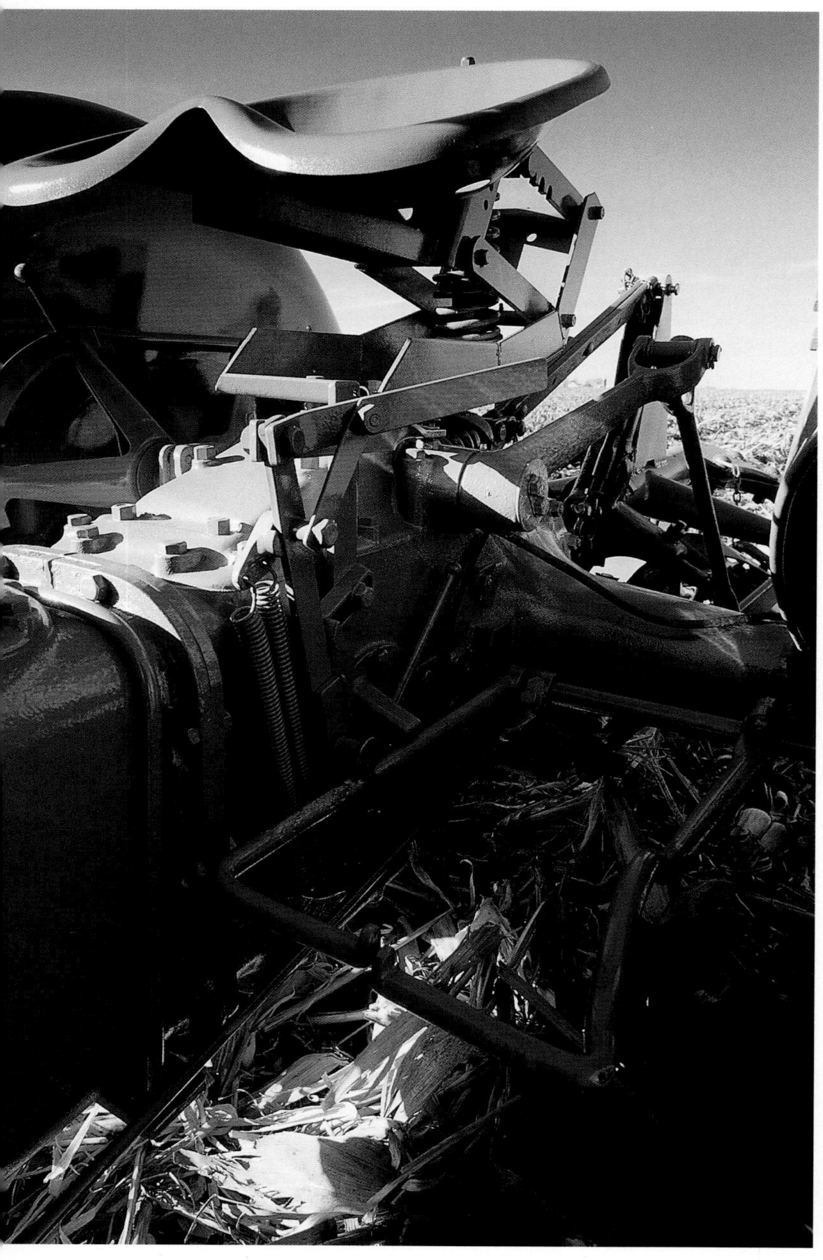

▴*Few tractor makers had as many aftermarket accessories available as Ford, again because of his unwillingness to make his own. This 2N, owned and restored by Dwight Emstrom of Galesburg, Illinois, has aftermarket steel sand lugs mounted outside the rear rubber tires as well as an aftermarket clutch mechanism that quickly disengages the clutch and operates both brakes if the plow hits a rock.*

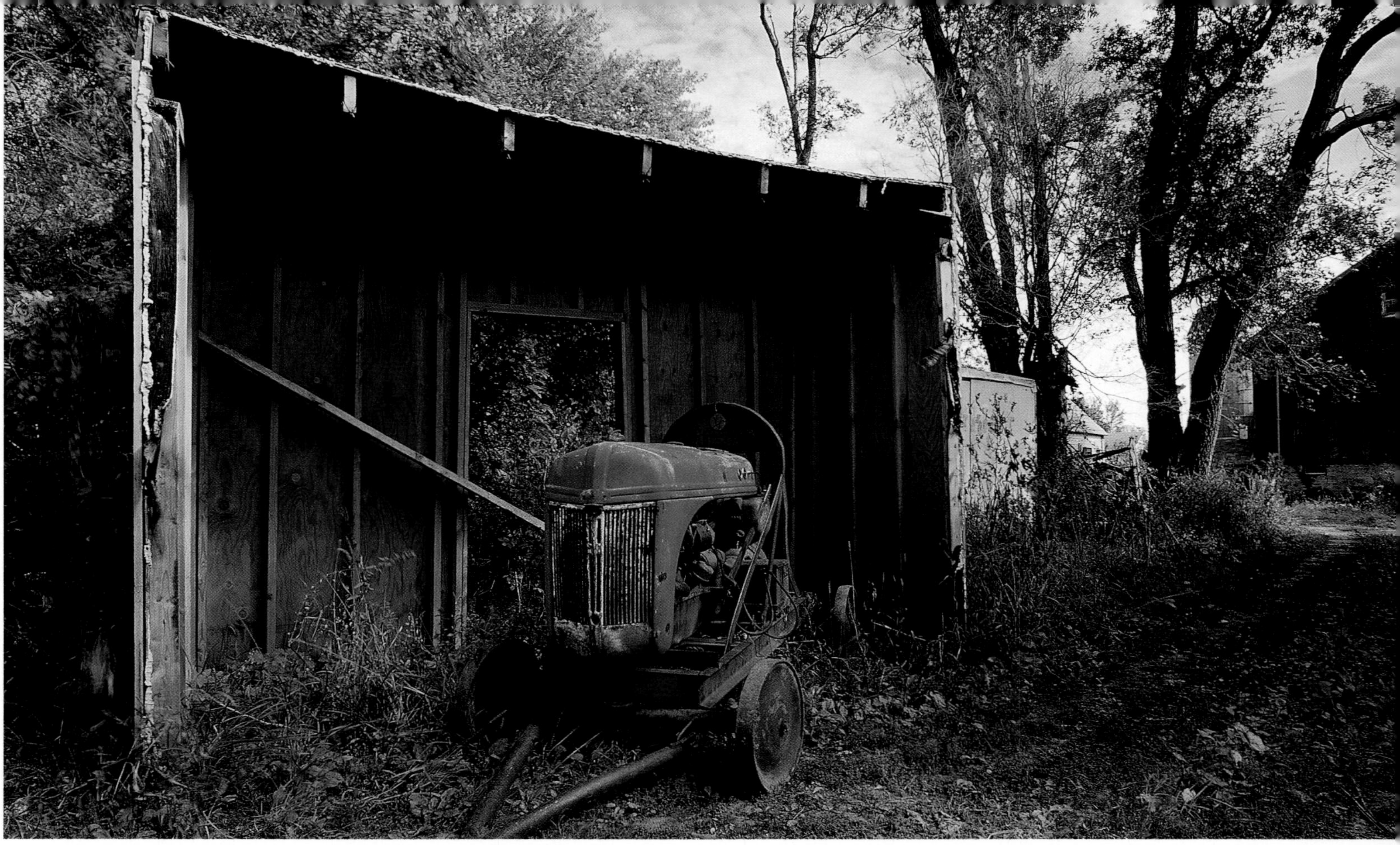

▲*The Ford 8N engine, tested in a tractor at the University of Nebraska in June 1950, measured 3.19inx3.75in. bore and stroke with a total capacity of 117.9ci. It was rated to run 1,750rpm at which it produced 17.7hp on the drawbar. Ford allowed engine speed to increase to 2,000rpm for belt pulley work and, in that application, the engine produced a maximum of 25.5hp with fuel efficiency measured at 11.2 horsepower hours per gallon consumed.*

▼*This was an early industrial application whose identity has long since rusted away. The 8N tractor engine was mounted onto channel iron rails and set on wheels. A clutch was fitted to the rear at the flywheel, and this was attached directly to the pump impeller. Performance and pump capacity cannot even be guessed, but it must be presumed that, if necessary, the engine moved a lot of water when it ran at 2,000rpm. This unique 1952 8N-6 Ford is owned by Palmer Fossum of Northfield, Minnesota.*

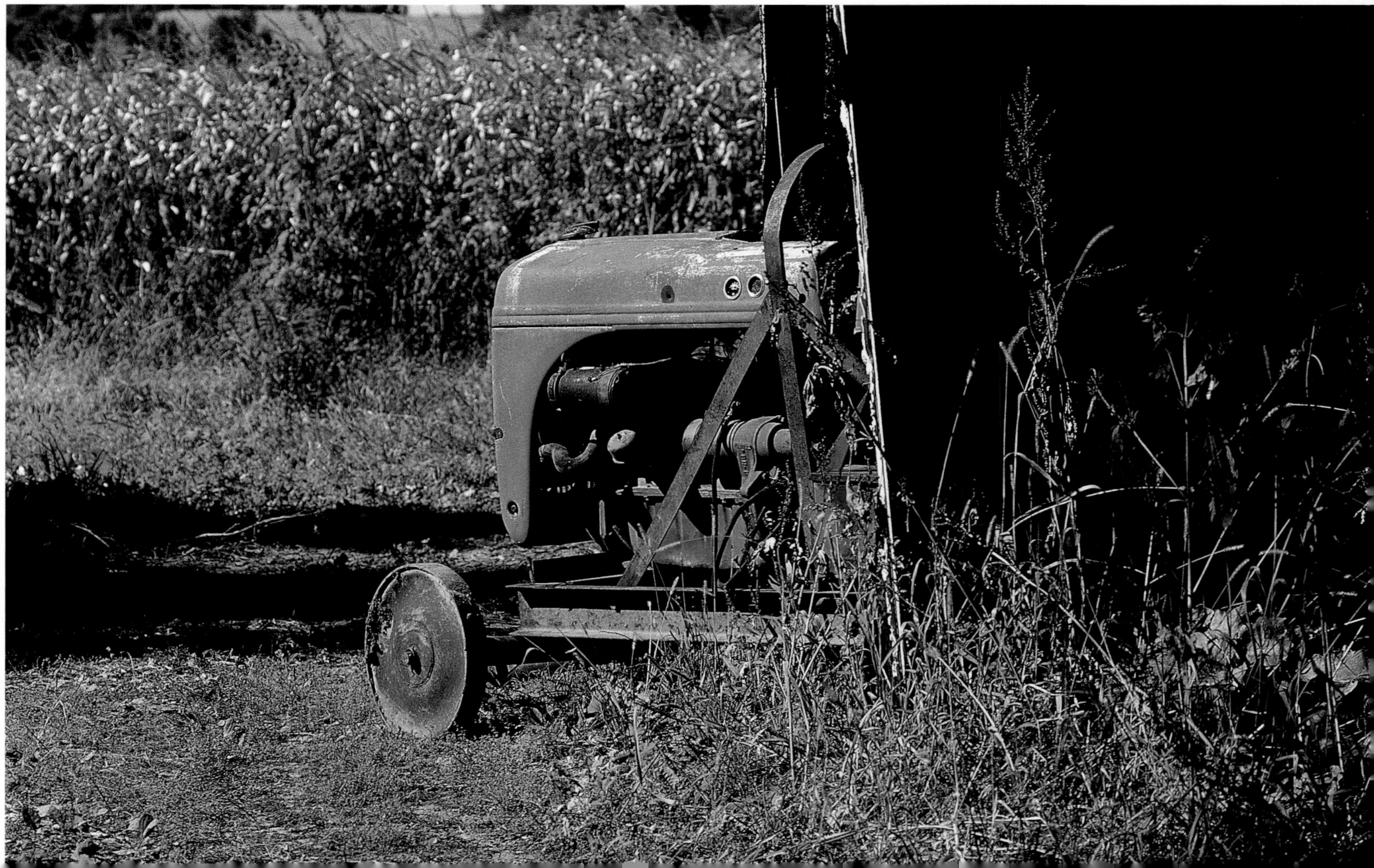

the farmer's seat. These gears were inefficient, generating as much heat as power. This heat transferred up to the farmer's steel seat. Later versions inverted the system and bathed the worm in oil, cooling the system and the farmer's backside. By 1920, Fordson's problems had largely been solved and sales, always steady, reached 70,000 near year end.

From his earliest tests, Ford hoped for a tractor-with-plow as a single unit. Current thinking still reflected the historical: The plow was hitched to the horse. No one thought that the plow could be part of the tractor. This was a new concept, as unit construction had been.

In Belfast, Ferguson had been working on such a plow. Using a Ford Model T with the Eros tractor conversion (among the better of the dozens of conversion kits available, this one came from St. Paul, Minnesota), he had a lightweight "tractor." Ferguson's wheel-less plow was nearly ready. In December 1917, he learned that a Ford tractor plant was planned for Cork. Until production was running, several thousand more Fordsons were to be imported.

Ferguson the showman looked at this as access to a much larger market for his plow. He grabbed his drawings and raced to London to meet Sorensen. Ferguson biographer Colin Fraser set the scene in his 1972 book, *Harry Ferguson: Inventor and Pioneer*: "'Your Fordson's all right as far as it goes,' Ferguson told Sorensen, 'but it doesn't really solve any of the fundamental problems.' Ferguson got Sorensen's attention. He unrolled his drawings and explained his theory that achieving efficient farm mechanization lay in equipment designed on the unit principle—that is to say the implement becoming part of the tractor when it was hitched on, but being readily detachable again."

This was exactly what Ford had said. And Sorensen's recollection in his biography in 1956, *My Forty Years With Ford*, was more that he had suggested Ford's idea to Ferguson. The unit idea ultimately changed tractor farming for good. From the start, Ferguson had shared with Henry the ambition of easing the farmer's workload, based on the same unpleasant experiences from childhood. Ferguson persevered, his greatest skill after engineering and salesmanship. The result was the Duplex hitch, a design beautiful and simple in its engineering. It was completed by the end of 1917. Viewed from the side, if the lines of the upper and lower arms were extended, they would have met several feet in front of the nose of the tractor. The effects of physical laws on this triangulated Duplex hitch meant that the drag on the plow always created downward pressure on the tractor. The greater the drag, the greater the down force.

An additional benefit of Ferguson's system was that not only could a lightweight tractor be used, but also the plow itself no longer needed to be of great weight. Its only drawback was that, as the tractor pivoted over changes in the field surface, the depth of the furrow changed opposite to what the front wheels did. There was no draft control.

After Sorensen's first meeting with Ferguson, both agreed to keep each other informed of developments. In 1920, Ferguson arranged a demonstration in Dearborn of his plow system to fit the Fordson.

The demonstration was a success, up to a point. The Ferguson plow performed admirably, but Ford and Ferguson had different goals in mind, different assessments of each other, and different views of their importance to each other. Ford thought Ferguson was an innovative and effective machinery salesman. He told Sorensen to hire him on the spot. Ferguson had no interest in working for anyone else. He wanted Ford to back him in a plant in Ireland. Ford dismissed the whole thing but offered to buy the patents from Ferguson. Ferguson politely refused. Both Ford and Ferguson knew that without a depth-control device the plow's usefulness was in doubt. Afterward, still in Dearborn, Ferguson contacted Eber Sherman, a New Yorker who was Ford's distributor for South America. Sherman agreed to handle sales of the plow and to help Ferguson find a manufacturer. Ferguson sailed home.

Ferguson's lack of success with Ford hurt. It brought his backers to their feet and knocked the inventor to his knees. After bitter disagreement, Ferguson resigned from Harry Ferguson, Ltd., and opened a new shop elsewhere in Belfast.

Back in the United States, Ford's Fordson was a continuing success.

Ford had entered the tractor business in 1917, and by 1921, he had hold of two-thirds of the entire market.

Ford had also succeeded in reacquiring majority interest in his automobile company, and he moved Ford & Son tractors into his new River Rouge plant. His Dearborn plant production had reached a record 399 a day, 10,248 for September. But the war ended. The River Rouge plant worked at capacity. It was too much. Overcapacity caught up. Sales in the 1920-21 depression dropped to 36,793 (though this was partly caused by new plant set-up time).

To keep production up, Ford cut the price of his tractor. Then he cut it again and again as he searched for the price level that would put the tractor in everyone's hands and keep his factories busy. Production had risen to nearly 69,000 in 1922, despite the economy, and to nearly 102,000 in 1923. A healthy export business continued, and between 1920 and 1926, nearly 25,000 were delivered to Russia. He took losses to meet those goals. The price war that resulted enraged and broke many competitors. But he had not only temporarily overwhelmed his competition, he had educated them.

In her book on International Harvester, *A Corporate Tragedy*, Barbara Marsh assessed Ford's impact. "The Fordson, much lighter than other tractors on the market, exemplified Detroit's know-how. It proved Harvester's engineers had a lot to learn about the refinements of internal combustion, heat treatment of steel, strength of materials and standardization of parts. Ford's example behooved Harvester and old-line makers of farm equipment to revamp their ancient production methods for the precision-machining requirements of the tractor. Reaping economies in production, Ford shattered the tractor industry, already undergoing a shake out, with repeated price slashing. By 1922, when the price on a Fordson dropped $230 to a level of $395, Ford effectively broadcast his willingness to lose money on tractors to keep production going."

International Harvester introduced its Farmall Regular as a direct result of Ford's Fordson. War was declared in the farm fields, and IHC's engineers went right to the front lines to test and improve their product. Implements dedicated specifically to the Farmall were introduced, and IHC's full-line dealers sold the system. Ford, still selling largely through his automobile dealers, had never recognized the value of his own implements.

Not only was there a profit incentive, but implements specifically meant for Fordsons would have better shown off the tractor's capabilities. Instead, farmers around the country made do

The ARPS tracks were all-steel offered in 13in (recommended for plowing to fit within the 14in furrow) or 16in widths. The track shoes were pressed steel with 1in grousers. A pneumatic rubber idler wheel kept track tension, using a 5.0x15in four-ply implement tire. Track width was adjustable at 52, 56, or 60in centers. Between 1920 and 1940, Arps produced more than 14,000 crawler and half-track kits.

Since he retired from active dairy farming in the early nineties, Palmer Fossum of Northfield, Minnesota, has made it his new job to gather and collect the most unusual pieces of Ford tractor history. His 1956 Model 650 is fitted with a Ford adjustable plow and the Blackhawk Half-Track manufactured by ARPS Corporation of New Holstein, Wisconsin.

The Tractor and Implement Division of Ford Motor Co., of Birmingham, Michigan, introduced the 600 series of tractors in 1955, to replace the two-year edition of the Jubilee. At the same time Ford also introduced the larger engine displacement 800 series. The 650 used Ford's 134ci inline four carried over from the Jubilee and hence, not specifically tested at Nebraska. However, the new tractor offered a five-speed transmission.

with Cockshutt, Oliver, or Deere plows or other attachments. When the Fordson failed to perform as advertised or expected, the mix of manufacturers was not blamed, the tractor was. Despite ever-falling prices, Fordson production declined, and by early 1928, Ford quit selling Fordsons in the United States. International Harvester had the lead again.

When Lord Percival Perry, head of the British Ford Motor Company, stopped in Dearborn on his annual visit, he saw stockpiles and silenced assembly lines. He seized the moment. He proposed to Sorensen (who was by now the head of tractor operations at Ford) that he, Perry, take the machinery and dies back to the United Kingdom. Perry would use them there to build tractors where they were still needed. Ford, who wanted development to continue on the unit plow and who preferred the automobile line had shut down instead of the tractor plant, agreed.

Ferguson continued his developments and even visited Ford several times during the twenties. He had nearly solved the draft control dilemma. A "floating skid" patent applied for in December 1923 worked in the interim. But still not satisfied, Ferguson adopted an internal on-board hydraulic-lift system to ease the chore of turning the tractor at the ends of rows. By adapting a sensor to the hydraulics, by replacing more rigid mounts with

▲ *Palmer Fossum mows his farm yard outside Northfield, Minnesota, with his Powermaster and a PTO-driven John Deere three-blade mower. The 1957 801 measured 66in tall, 72in wide, and 133in overall on an 85in wheelbase. It operated on 5.50x16in front tires and 12.0x28in rear tires.*

ball joints, and by increasing the angle of the top strut (now a single instead of a pair), he closed in on the perfection he sought.

In 1925, he had incorporated in the United States with Eber and George Sherman, as Ferguson-Sherman, Inc., to manufacture and market his plow. In 1928, his new three-point hitch with automatic draft control was ready. Yet Ford was switching over his Dearborn plant to production of his new Model A automobile. Ferguson was caught again without a manufacturer. And then it was 1929. The stock market crashed, and the Great Depression began.

Ferguson did not give up. Reasoning that, in tight money times, it might be easier to sell something if a manufacturer could see it in the flesh (or at least in steel), Ferguson ordered parts to build a prototype tractor and unit plow. Transmission pieces came from Britain's largest gear producer, David Brown Co. The engine, a four-cylinder Hercules, came from the United States. The tractor began to come together in Belfast, and when complete, Ferguson ordered it painted black. Some say it was because of Henry Ford's dictum that only black was suitable for cars. But it is equally likely that Ferguson, who had so little tolerance for unnecessary frills, looked on black as the most proper, unadorned finish. It was only later, seeing how field dirt contrasted against the black, that he changed to gray paint.

The black tractor went into tests, but a draft control problem leftover from the Fordson still existed. An experiment proved that instead of using the hydraulic cylinder oil under pressure on the bottom two links to position the plow and control its draft, it worked better to use the hydraulics on top to lift the plow by compressing the cylinder and letting gravity take the plow down.

Ferguson had succeeded. Now a manufacturer was needed. Ferguson took to the road again, this time staying in the United Kingdom. Gear maker David Brown became a tractor manufacturer, and the first Brown-Ferguson machines rolled out in early 1936. Demonstrations quickly quieted farmers' skepticism in the United Kingdom.

Ferguson invited Eber Sherman to one of his demonstrations. He hoped that Sherman would tell Henry Ford about the new machine and Ferguson's hopes for vast worldwide production.

"What the world needs right now," historian Allan Nevins quoted Henry Ford in the fall of 1937, "is a good tractor that will sell for around $250." Sherman returned to Dearborn as Ferguson's emissary for just such a machine, and in late 1938, Ferguson and a small staff took a Ferguson-Brown to Fair Lane. Ford had only reluctantly ceased tractor production ten years earlier. Fordson production continued first in Cork, then after 1933, in Dagenham, England. Yet Ford was thinking of a new model for

North American sales. Several models had been developed, one a three-wheel row-crop type with Ford's flathead V-8; another was a four-wheel standard in which Ford wanted an overdrive road gear. But Ford was dissatisfied with his own engineers' work.

Ferguson's timing was perfect. His new tractor finished its demonstration. Ford was quiet, but soon offered again to buy Ferguson's patents. Ferguson replied that Ford didn't have enough money and they weren't for sale anyway.

It remains one of the great business stories of modern history that these two men, each stubborn and distrusting of written contracts, would consummate a deal so grand and important out of doors, in private, out of earshot of witnesses, and simply on a shake of the hands.

A gentlemen's agreement. Colin Fraser reported the terms: "Ferguson would be responsible for all design and engineering matters; Ford would manufacture the tractor and assume all risks involved in manufacture; Ferguson would distribute the tractors, which Ford would deliver; either party could terminate the arrangement at any time without obligation to the other, for any reason whatever, even if it was only 'because he didn't like the color of his hair'; and the Ford tractor plant in Britain [at Dagenham] would ultimately build the Ferguson System tractor on similar terms to those established for Dearborn."

All agreed to and sealed with a handshake.

Ferguson was overjoyed. Ford was excited. But it was a short honeymoon. Sorensen's recollections were clear. "When Ferguson appeared in 1938, we were ready with a new tractor, and his plow with a hydraulic lifting device appealed to Mr. Ford...We wanted him to adapt a plow to our tractor. We did not need him to show us how to build tractors—he needed us. We did want him to come with us because we knew we would make a success of his plow if we could adapt it."

Allan Nevins' history emphasized it was Ford, not Ferguson, making design decisions and specifications. Ford invested $12 million in tooling costs and helped Ferguson finance his new distribution company, Sherman having dissolved Ferguson-Sherman Manufacturing.

The 9N, the Ford Tractor with Ferguson System was introduced June 29, 1939. Its $585 price included rubber tires, power take-off, Ferguson hydraulics, electric starter, generator, and battery (lights were optional). The gasoline four-cylinder had an automobile-type muffler, and 9N sales brochures showed possible mounting points for a radio, due to the quietness of the engine.

Ford's 9N improved upon the cantankerous Fordson by updating the ignition with a distributor and coil. An innovative system of tire mounts for the rear wheels and versatile axle mounts for the fronts enabled farmers to accommodate any width row-crop work they needed, from 48 to 76in, using nothing more than the supplied wrench and jack. This may have been a Ferguson invention since it disappeared from the 8N tractors. But then, so did the Ferguson System badge on the Ford's radiator.

Ford aimed for the perfect tractor with his 9N. He had tried before with the Fordson and believed he had it right by the time he introduced his new model in 1939. Still, there were problems with his newest effort, some of them matters of operator comfort and convenience. With the introduction late in 1942 of the 2N, several changes occurred because of wartime needs for metal and rubber. Chrome instrument bezels, battery covers, and radiator caps all went to steel in '41.

Ferguson again was a victim of timing and a new world war caused orders for the 9N to reach little more than half the original projection: 35,742 instead of 63,750. Production nearly touched 43,000 in 1941, but wartime rationing of rubber returned all tractors to steel wheels. The lower output raised Ford's costs, and eventually the price followed.

Still, until the 2N arrived to replace it, the 9N made significant impact on the farmer, as Ford and Ferguson had hoped. And it demonstrated the engineering ideas Harry Ferguson had struggled to prove for decades.

Just before the Second World War, more than 6.8 million families in the United States still lived on farms. Only 1.2 million had tractors while, according to a U.S. Department of Agriculture study, 17 million horses still worked the farms. Nearly one-fifth of the land under cultivation in North America was devoted to feeding the draft animals, which needed to eat year round, a fact recited regularly by Ferguson and Ford.

In 1948, Ford introduced the 8N. Ferguson's name was nowhere to be found. Known throughout England as a feisty, opinionated inventor, his outspoken nature and his strong belief in his correctness put many people off, some of them in positions to do him great good. He had rankled Sorensen. The directors of Ford Motor Company, Ltd., refused to seat him or to manufacture his tractor while their own Fordson continued to sell well.

The "Handshake Agreement" proved as good as the paper it was written on. Both sides eventually cheated on it.

When Henry's son, Edsel, died in 1943, the senior Ford, then eighty, returned to the company to run it. His grandson, Henry II, who was twenty-six, was called home from the Navy to take over. He learned that the tractor operation had already lost $20 million. (The U.S. Office of Price Administration had allowed no price increases by any manufacturer during the war.) To watch expenses more closely, Ford returned tractor operations to Highland Park from the Rouge plant.

At the same time, Henry Ford hoped to clarify his agreement with Ferguson. After frustrating Ford the man and Ford the company, Ferguson returned home and left things for his company's president to handle. Sorensen had characterized Ferguson as a "stand-by consultant" to Lord Perry. In 1946, Ford Motor Company tried to buy into Ferguson or buy him out, to form a new sales and distribution company. Ferguson's temper rose at the final offer, thirty percent of the new company and no royalties on his patents.

Negotiations broke. Effective December 31, 1946, Ford's agreement with Ferguson would end. Ford was to continue to manufacture tractors through June 1947 for Ferguson to market, but Ford immediately established its own distribution company, the Dearborn Motor Corporation.

Then Henry Ford died on Monday, April 7, 1947, at age eighty-three. In his lifetime, he had sent 1.7 million tractors out of his factory doors with his name on them.

The refusal of Ford Motor Company, Ltd., to manufacture Ferguson's tractor had led him outside by this time. A 2N clone, the Ferguson TE-20, went into production in Coventry, England. It used a Lucas electrical system, and its engine had overhead valves and a four-speed transmission, improvements Ferguson advocated for the 9N and 2N but which Dearborn had not yet picked up.

In July 1947, right after Ford's last shipments to Ferguson, the new 8N was introduced. It boasted some twenty improvements over the 2N, including a four-speed transmission. It came equipped with the Ferguson System. No royalties were paid.

Ford 801 POWER

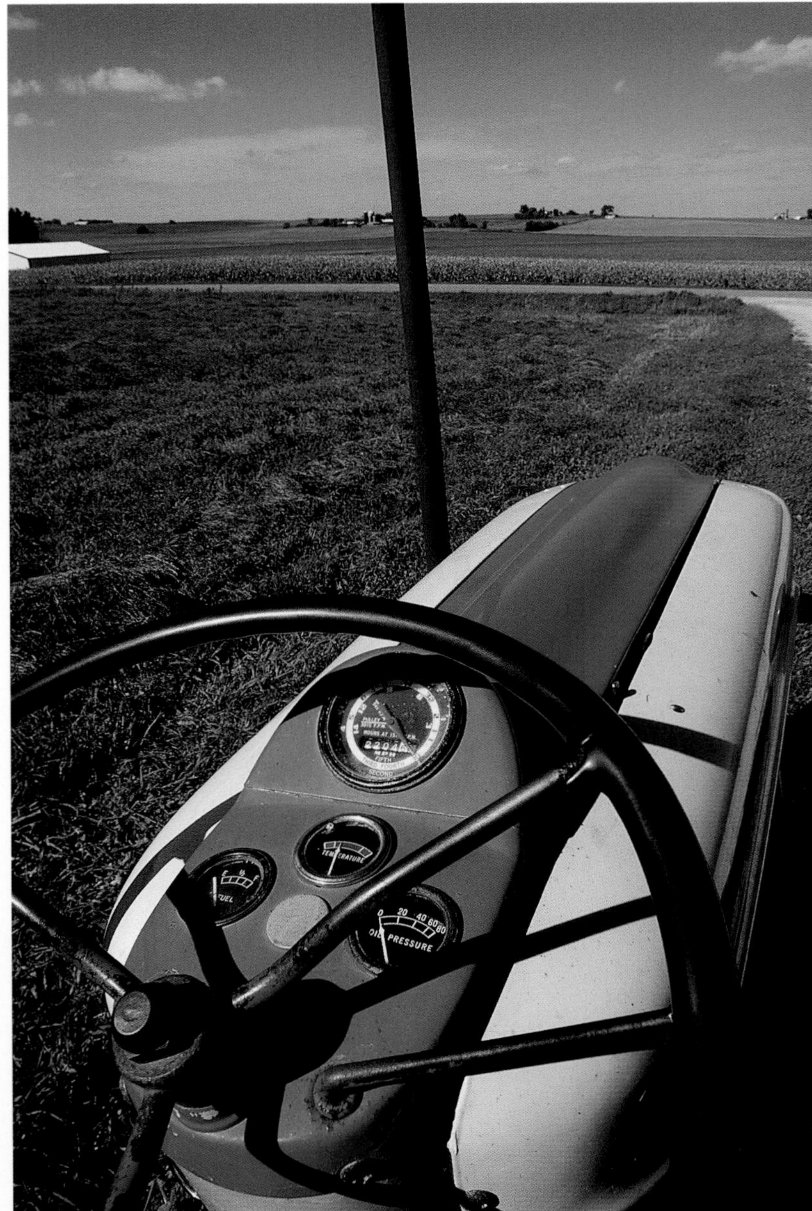

▲*The 801 Powermaster-series tractors were three- or four-plow rated machines. These were offered as gasoline, LPG, or diesel-engine versions. A twenty-amp generator recharged the six-volt battery and electrical system. Electric lights were standard, and an optional lighting kit put implement lights on the rear fenders.*

◂*The "Red Tiger" Powermaster engine had a bore and stroke of 3.90x3.60in for total capacity of 172ci. Ford used the same block for LPG and diesel fuel as well. Engine output was 31.9 drawbar horsepower and a maximum of 45.7 brake horsepower. A five-speed transmission was used that provided a top speed in road gear of nearly 12mph. Power steering was standard.*

▸▸*This 600-series Ford was equipped with only a single-point hitch. Of course, this one also had a transmission oil cooler, front and rear fenders, a full cab with white reflector tape, and a rotating amber safety beam on the roof. This was not standard equipment in reaction to the Ford-Ferguson breakup. It was meant for use by the U.S. Air Force an airplane tug. It is difficult to know now just how many were produced but the "Mototug" was common throughout U.S. Air Force and National Guard bases through the sixties.*

37

LIGHT SWITCH

◂*This three-door cab—one sliding door on each side plus a hinged door at the rear—provided seating for three as well. Two tool boxes beneath the rear windows served as jump seats. A torque-converter transmission made best use of the maximum 22.4 drawbar horsepower from the Ford Industrial four-cylinder 134ci engine. A huge heater/defroster kept the operator warm and the windows clear through the winter. This curious Ford is another part of the collection belonging to Palmer Fossum in Northfield, Minnesota.*

Ferguson immediately set out to produce a tractor for the United States. His TE-20 was to have a cousin in the colonies, the TO-20. But his financing dried up. Potential investors worried over Ferguson's ability to compete against the power and size of Ford. He approached other car makers, Willys-Overland, Kaiser-Frazer, and even General Motors.

But GM disagreed over the size of the tractor the U.S. farmer needed, and Willys would agree only if it had controlling interest. Ferguson, more and more riled by this time, directed his wrath at Ford.

"It'll be a grand fight" Harry Ferguson said, as he filed suit against Ford. He claimed damages of $251 million. He charged "conspiracy" to infringe on patents, to willfully destroy his distribution business, and to block manufacture of its own tractor. Ford denied or repudiated every allegation. The legal battle, now not merely a patent suit but also an antitrust suit, dragged on for four years. More than one million pages of evidence were taken, nearly 11,000 from Ferguson himself.

Meanwhile, Ferguson began producing his TO-20 in Detroit. By the end of 1948, he had recorded a profit of more than $500,000; 100 tractors a day rolled out the doors. So Ford counter-sued Ferguson in July 1949, charging him with "conspiracy" to dominate the world tractor market and ruin Ford Motor Company. Ford hoped to wear Ferguson down. The opposite occurred. When the suit came to trial in March 1951, Ferguson added $90 million more to cover the Ford tractors built since filing the suit.

The trial dragged on for months. It did wear Ferguson down. On July 17, 1951, he told his lawyers to accept a settlement if Ford offered. Ferguson, exhausted, had spent $3.5 million and received $9.25 million on April 9, 1952. Ferguson's patents on much of the three-point hitch had run out by the time the suit was settled. The remaining pieces still covered had to be redesigned by Ford. But Ford was already at work developing its next tractor.

Ford's fiftieth anniversary in 1953 was commemorated with the new NAA tractor that began production shortly after the new year began. Substantially restyled, it was officially named the Golden Jubilee 1903-1953 Model but quickly became known as the Jubilee. The 8N had grown some to become the Jubilee. It was 4in longer and higher and about 100lb heavier. It also introduced Ford's new Red Tiger engine, an overhead-valve four. A new vane-type hydraulic pump replaced the Ferguson System pump, and it was relocated to the right rear of the engine. Live power take-off was optional. The Jubilee, a three-plow tractor, was produced until 1955, when Ford changed its tractor direction.

Until the introduction of the new 600 and 800 series, five tractors in all in 1955, Ford had been a one-tractor company since 1917. Now Ford, which had on and off again held the major market share, could compete more effectively against all its opponents.

LPG, liquefied petroleum gas, became a fuel option in the United States and United Kingdom, and diesel engines were available for the Fordson Major. Workmaster and Powermaster tractors were introduced in 1958, with model series numbers from 601 through 901. Diesel engines also came to the United States in 1958. In 1959, Ford introduced its "Select-o-Speed" transmission on its 881 model, using hydraulic power for gear change in an automatic-type transmission.

In the year of Ford's Golden Jubilee, Harry Ferguson fulfilled his childhood wish of immigrating to Canada. In 1953, he sold his tractor and plow company to Massey-Harris in Ontario. Automobiles once again piqued his interests, and most of the proceeds of the sale, $16 million, were invested into acquiring rights for the torque converter and all-wheel-drive systems.

Harry Ferguson died on October 26, 1960. Less than three months before, he had contacted friends about a new idea—about getting back into the game. He wanted to build a new tractor, a tractor that would make use of the torque converter automatic transmission and four-wheel drive.

Chapter Nine

A Brief History of Tractor Innovation

Design and Engineering Broaden Their Impact

IT TOOK THE HUMAN RACE THOUSANDS OF years to advance agriculture beyond animal power. Beginning in the mid-nineteenth century, the inventors and tinkerers of the previous 200 years would have seen their ideas put to practical use. But the next evolutionary cycle took only a fraction as long. It was not even seventy-five years before things changed again.

From the late 1880s to the late twenties, the farm tractor manufacturing industry evolved steadily. It switched from primarily steam engine power for stationary, portable, and traction engine applications, to the gasoline engine. The importance of engineering became clear to manufacturers as they changed their products from steam to gas. With the arrival of tractor testing, the role of the engineer was enlarged even more. The buying public began to recognize its own power. Manufacturers could, of course, provide a "ringer" tractor, a hopped-up, cheater machine for the tests. But results achieved on the dirt test oval at the University of Nebraska were expected in the potato fields in Maine and wheat lands of California. Predictability and dependability were performance characteristics that advanced tractors beyond the capabilities of backyard tinkerers and early-day blacksmiths.

The next change was even more dramatic, though the machines looked little different. Eleven years after the first Nebraska tests, Caterpillar demonstrated reliable, practical diesel power. Soon after its 1931 introduction, just as with gas and steam before it, diesel power became available for stationary, portable, and tractor applications. However, the engineering of the diesel was even more critical. The difficulty of starting engines using the gelatinous fuel on a cold morning necessitated pure engineering solutions. It took some companies until the late fifties to feel confident enough of their engineering and trusting enough of farmer demand for it to offer diesel engines. By this time, some of the diesel pioneers had already phased out all the other fuels from their product line-up.

▲*The YT used one-half of a Minneapolis-Moline four-cylinder engine to make a two-cylinder engine. Crudely cut cylinder heads topped the three prototypes while this head is more finished in appearance with head bolts being further into the casting than at the edges in the prototypes. The carburetor was a Schebler TR while the magneto was a Fairbanks Morse Model FMJ.*

▸*The YT measured 80in tall to the top of the stack, 80in wide, and 119in long overall on a 79in wheelbase. The transmission was a four-speed-forward/one-speed-reverse gearbox similar to later Model Rs. Front tires were 7.50x10 while rears were 9.50x38s. Engine specifications are pretty much unknown as it appears that nearly all but a few of the twenty-five versions built were recalled to the factory and probably destroyed or adapted to other experimental units.*

After diesel engines, the next step in the evolution was much more noticeable; yet, it occurred within seven years of the new power. A new breed of engineer became involved—the industrial designer. These people were part sheet metal designer, part manufacturing specialist, part marketing researcher, part aesthetician, part structural engineer, part agricultural engineer, part orthopedic surgeon, part magician, and part miracle worker. At first, this amalgam was brought in simply to make one manufacturer's tractors stand out from all the rest, to become "more salable" than the competition.

In 1938, Deere & Co. introduced "styled" tractors. By 1950, every major company manufacturing tractors in North America had hired industrial designers and engineers as outside consultants or as inside staff.

In *Webster's New World Dictionary*, an "engineer" is described, among other ways, as "a person who operates or supervises the operation of engines or technical equipment; a specialist in planning and directing operations in some technical field." That these individuals began to work on tractors is obvious. It is the definition of "engineering" that is more apropos: it is "the science concerned with putting scientific knowledge to practical uses...; the planning, designing, construction, or management of machinery..., etc."

This is most accurately what happened to farm tractors from the early 1900s through the early sixties.

Alvin Lombard's Log Hauler, his turn-of-the-century steam traction engine crawler, fed its steam from the boiler equally to each side's compound, two-cylinder,

MM
MINNEAPOLIS-MOLINE

◂*The 1937 YT was a curiosity. Three prototypes were built as development mules before a limited production run of another twenty-two was completed. Each was given a U.S. Army Air Force serial number, this one being #52815. But whether it was meant to be an aircraft tug or something else, it never went into regular production. This experimental tractor was restored and is owned by Walter and Bruce Keller of Kaukauna, Wisconsin.*

◂◂*Experimental models are prized by collectors for their rarity and mystery. Each company builds models it never puts into regular series production. For reasons of inadequate performance, insufficient interest or demand from the marketplace, or just a simple change of mind, the limited edition tractors are tested, prodded, measured, and, then, all the evidence of their existence is generally destroyed.*

vertical engines. There was only one throttle valve for all four cylinders, located in the dome. There were no track clutches or track brakes to slow one side to assist in turning the 19ft-long, 18-ton, 100hp engine. It was all accomplished by the tillerman on the wood bench mounted above the front skis. Freezing in the winter, sitting ahead of the boiler, he cranked the worm-and-sector steering gear to change direction of the lumber train behind him. Lombard's Log Hauler had no compressor or air brakes. He expected that friction—even on ice—would stop the crawler and its loads even when tugging sleds loaded with twenty tons of logs each. When Ben Holt adopted the Lombard crawler technology, he added track clutches and brakes to more efficiently maneuver, or to stop, his 23ft-long, tiller-wheel, gas-engined crawlers.

The English tractor, the Field Marshal Diesel, was started simply. One method used a shotgun shell slipped into the cylinder head and triggered when the cylinder was full of fuel and just past top dead center. But this was hard on main bearings. The other technique called for removing the T-handle near the head (it's hollow on the inside end) and placing a wick soaked in diesel fuel inside it, setting a match to the wick and letting it burn until it glowed hot. Inserting it back into the engine, the operator opened the compression relief valves and started pulling on the massive 24x5in flywheel. This method needed two strong men. Once the compression built up, the machine would pop to life.

Deere's diesel, and those that came before it and since—Caterpillar, IHC, Allis-Chalmers, White, and Ford—accomplished the same complicated tasks much more easily. Deere and Caterpillar mounted a small gasoline-powered engine on the diesel engine block. Its exhaust was vented through the larger diesel block to preheat the cylinders, and then, when the larger engine was sufficiently warmed, the smaller gas engine was engaged by clutch to turn over the diesel, building compression until it popped to life.

Power take-off (PTO) was at first reliant on tractor forward motion for its power shaft drive to rear-mounted implements. When it first appeared in 1929 as independent, or "live," PTO on International Harvester Model 10-20 prototypes, it was a complicated, cumbersome, dangerous, and ugly affair, operated by a clutch off the front of the crankcase. A pulley wheel ran to a chain that drove a shaft along the side of the engine. The shaft ran back to a bevel gear at the belt pulley that was connected internally to the PTO shaft. With the front clutch engaged, the belt pulley and the PTO shaft ran at the same time. IHC never marketed it.

It would be another eighteen years before live PTO would be commercially available. Engineered and introduced by the Canadian manufacturer Cockshutt for its 1947 models, their system coupled the PTO shaft to its own clutch within the transmission housing. No longer would harvesters or binders or any other shaft-driven implement slow or stop its function when the tractor slowed or stopped.

World War II interrupted regular production as tractor makers were drafted to produce tanks and artillery shells and guns. Just as during World War I, a variety of metals, particularly bronze, copper, chromium, and steel, came into short supply for civilian purposes. Tractors and implements that might have otherwise been discarded and replaced were repaired.

Recognizing that many rural males—more hired men than farmers—had gone to war, companies such as International Harvester organized programs and classes where rural women were taught to operate and maintain the equipment. Posters and advertising encouraged women to become the "field artillery," to become a "tractorette," as their urban counterparts had become Rosie the Riveter. Women hated the nicknames but rose to the challenge. One study in Kansas in 1943 showed women performing 85 percent of the farm machinery operation. Frequently farm women, adept at operating tractors, planters, and harvesters, hired townswomen to take care of their home, cleaning and preparing meals while they performed the field work for their absent husbands.

When the war ended, it took about a year to reconvert factories to tractor production. A great deal of equipment was back-ordered, and the establishment of the Marshall Plan only made matters worse. Existing, quality manufacturers worked frantically engineering ways to produce machinery faster. A number of new manufacturers jumped quickly into the business, shipping tractors overseas. Companies like General Tractor in Seattle, Intercontinental Manufacturing near Dallas, Implement Manufacturing Co. of Ogden, Utah, and Jumbo Steel Products of suburban Los Angeles appeared. Businesses were born named after founders, cities, days of the week, and emotional states: Long Manufacturing, Detroit Tractor with an all-wheel-drive model, the Friday Tractor Co., and Love Tractor, Inc., with a variable-speed machine capable of 42mph.

Companies popped up with odd configurations, unusual innovations, and unnatural engine choices. R. H. Sheppard brought out tractors with two- and three-cylinder diesels. Metal Parts Corporation produced its Haas "Atomic" with a one-cylinder airplane engine. National Implement Company offered its Harris Power Horse four-wheel drive. General Tractor Corporation manufactured its Powerbilt four-wheel drive that actually used the load shifting on the drawbar to help turn the tractor. Still others bore names that hinted at competence despite where they might be headquartered. Custom Manufacturing Co., National Implement Co., and the Earthmaster Farm Equipment Co. entered the postwar market boom, joining Farmaster Corporation with its offices in New York City and Global Trading Corporation with its offices in Washington, D.C. Each of these appeared with tractors that were of lesser or greater quality. But many of these disappeared soon after the major manufacturers caught up to back orders and began shipping overseas again.

Among major North American tractor makers, design and engineering improved the seats and reinvented the transmissions with developments like the torque amplifier on International Harvester tractors. Disc brakes appeared on Olivers, improved implement hitches and power take-off were offered on Cases with the Eagle Hitch, Allis-Chalmers introduced its Traction Booster, and four-wheel drive was finally tamed by the Wagner Brothers of Portland through the adoption of a key hinge.

▲The Full Crawler Company, a department of George M. Smith Steel Casting Company of Milwaukee, Wisconsin produced only a handful of these conversion kits for Fordsons. A number of companies produced add-on half-track adaptations for the Fordson and a company called Snow Motors Inc., of Detroit, Michigan, even produced a pair of spiral cylinders as a replacement for wheels for use in deep soft snow.

Aftermarket specialty makers introduced LPG conversion kits, do-it-yourself power-steering hydraulic systems for most tractors, and even turbocharger kits for many diesel makes. By the end of the 1950s, Harry Ferguson's three-point hitch had been adopted by the American Society of Agricultural Engineers and the Society of Automotive Engineers as the Category I standard system. This vindicated for all time any question of Ferguson's contribution to mechanized agriculture.

The end of the fifties was most notable for the first of engineering experiments with alternative engines. Ford startled the competitions' engineers and farmers alike with its experimental Typhoon, a free piston turbine engine coupled to Ford's Power-Shift semi-automatic transmission. This was first shown in 1957. Then in 1959, Allis-Chalmers showed off its fuel-cell tractor, an experimental model powered by what was basically 1,008 electric fuel cells, similar to wet-cell batteries.

Researchers at Iowa State University worked with Ford to produce a "tandem-hitch" tractor, which in its most manageable version mated one tractor without front axle or wheels to the rear of another in front of it. This system, first shown in 1960, provided more drawbar power, but conversion and operation was cumbersome. Deere & Co.'s solution to farmer requests for more power was an eight-year-long secret effort by engineers and industrial designers working out of a former grocery. In the end, Deere retired its long-cherished two-cylinder tractors and introduced four- and six-cylinder in-line, upright diesels in new sheet metal. At the end of an event- and technology-filled 1960, heavy-truck maker White Motor Co. of Cleveland, Ohio, acquired Oliver, overnight entering the tractor and implement business.

A year later, Allis-Chalmers introduced its first turbocharged diesel, its engineers controlling the power and the problems experienced by dozens of do-it-yourself engineers on the family farm. And International Harvester showed its experimental gas turbine engine coupled to its hydrostatic transmission. The startling-looking tractor, roughly the size of a Farmall 200, its body of fiberglass, was powered by an engine that weighed only 60lb, turned at 57,000rpm, measured 21in long, and produced 80hp. In early 1962, White added Cockshutt Farm Machinery to its holdings, and in 1963, it acquired Minneapolis-Moline. The same year, engineer Vernon Roosa, working in New York City, introduced his rotary-type, diesel fuel-injection pump to replace the much larger and mechanically more complicated in-line

▲ *Ford's own in-line four-cylinder engine powered the Full Crawler version. Bore and stroke of the Ford measured 4.0x5.0in. At the rated speed of 1,000rpm, peak drawbar horsepower was 12.3 while belt pulley output was a maximum of 22.3. However, horsepower loss through the gearing and track drive would have been considerable. This 1924 machine is owned by Mrs. Edith Heidrick of Woodland, California.*

▲*The original jeep of 1938 resembled a U-DLX without the cab. Four-wheel drive was added by 1940, and the operator was moved more to the center of the vehicle. Minneapolis-Moline's Jeep measured 58in tall to the top of the steering wheel, 77in wide, and 166in long from front hook to the rear one. It was built on a 100in wheelbase. It rode on 9.0x10 10-ply truck tires. The four-cylinder engine used Delco electrics and a Schebler TR carburetor. This 1944 Jeep is owned by Walter and Bruce Keller of Kaukauna, Wisconsin.*

▸*While nearly every company produced Jeeps during the War, history seems pretty well set on Minneapolis-Moline producing the first vehicle called a "Jeep". While it was being tested at Minnesota National Guard Camp Ripley, the ability of this machine to go anywhere reminded some observers of a Popeye the Sailor cartoon creature with similar characteristics, called Jeep. The name stuck even when Ford built prototypes and Willys-Overland-built hundreds of thousands for the armed forces.*

▲*Raymond Johnson of Fremont, Nebraska was famous for racing a Jumbo Simpson at county and state fairs! With a ten-speed-plus-overdrive transmission, he routinely averaged 60mph to win. He even was stopped once for speeding on a Nebraska highway at 70mph. The Jumbo used hydraulic brakes, necessary for Johnson's kind of driving. The 217ci Chrysler engine had bore and stroke of 4.25x4.375. At 1,200rpm, nearly 35hp was available on the drawbar.*

▸*With its front-hinged engine cover, servicing virtually anything up front was very easy. The Simpson ran on gasoline but could be fitted to operate on kerosene for $125. The PTO and belt-pulley were another $175, and a live onboard hydraulic system was $395. Jumbo also manufactured land scrapers and land levelers and other pre-planting implements. This tractor was restored and is owned by Raynard Schmidt of Vail, Iowa.*

JUMBO
GAS

▲*This tractor was manufactured in suburban Los Angeles by the Jumbo Steel Products Company of Azusa, California. Jumbo used a Chrysler industrial type 5A-210 engine that gave farmers throughout North America the benefit of going to a local Chrysler dealer for service. Jumbo's Model B row-crop tractor and Model C standard tread tractor sold for $2,050 in 1948. Jumbo produced its first tractor in 1946 and was out of the tractor business by mid-1955. This was the 1946 Model B.*

pumps that fed each cylinder individually with their own fuel pump. Soon after, Roosa introduced his "Master Pencil Nozzle," a smaller, simpler nozzle, better suited to the more prevalent direct-injection-type diesel engines that were overtaking the precombustion chamber head versions.

Following decades of complaints by wives and widows about farm tractor safety, Deere & Co. introduced the Roll-Gard rollover protection system, developed by its own engineers working intensely with Henry Dreyfuss & Associates. Unable to give it away to farmers who were too sure that tragedy would happen only to the other guy, Deere gave the technology to its competitors. No sooner was that safety issue addressed than concern over slow-moving vehicles surfaced. The Automotive Safety Foundation, monitoring the numerous rear-end accidents in which fast-moving automobiles hit slow-moving tractors, funded the creation and subsequent standardization of the fluorescent yellow and orange triangle, developed at Ohio State University by agricultural engineering graduate student Kenneth Harkness.

During this period, up through 1965—and the decades since then—Webster's definition of engineering has been a synonym for tractor development. Yet it has been the goal of everyone from Otto von Guericke to Nicolaus Otto to Rudolf Diesel to practice engineering: "The science concerned with putting scientific knowledge to practical uses."

▲*The row crop was delivered on 5.50x16in front tires and 10x38in rears. It stood 65in tall, 78in wide, and 129in long overall, on an 85in wheelbase. It weighed 3,000lb dry. The Dodge truck transmission offered five forward speeds with a top speed of 22.4mph. Rear track was adjustable. Jumbo used Chrysler automobile wheels and spindles on the front and a Dodge two-ton truck rear end.*

▲*The 1948 Model E used a Wisconsin Model TF in-line air-cooled two-cylinder engine. With bore and stroke of 3.25x3.25in, total capacity was 53.9ci and Gibson rated the engine as 12.6hp at 2,000rpm. A Bendix 0.75in carburetor and a Fairbanks-Morse FMJ magneto were standard equipment. This little machine is owned by Paul Brecheisen of Helena, Ohio.*

▶*It's as small as it looks. It stands 72in tall to the top of the exhaust, 72in wide, 96in long overall, and its wheelbase is barely 68in. It weighed less than 1,900lb. It operated on 4.0x12in front tires and 8.0x24in rears. A three-speed transmission allowed a top speed of 7mph. Gibson Corporation was located in Longmont, Colorado.*

GIBSON

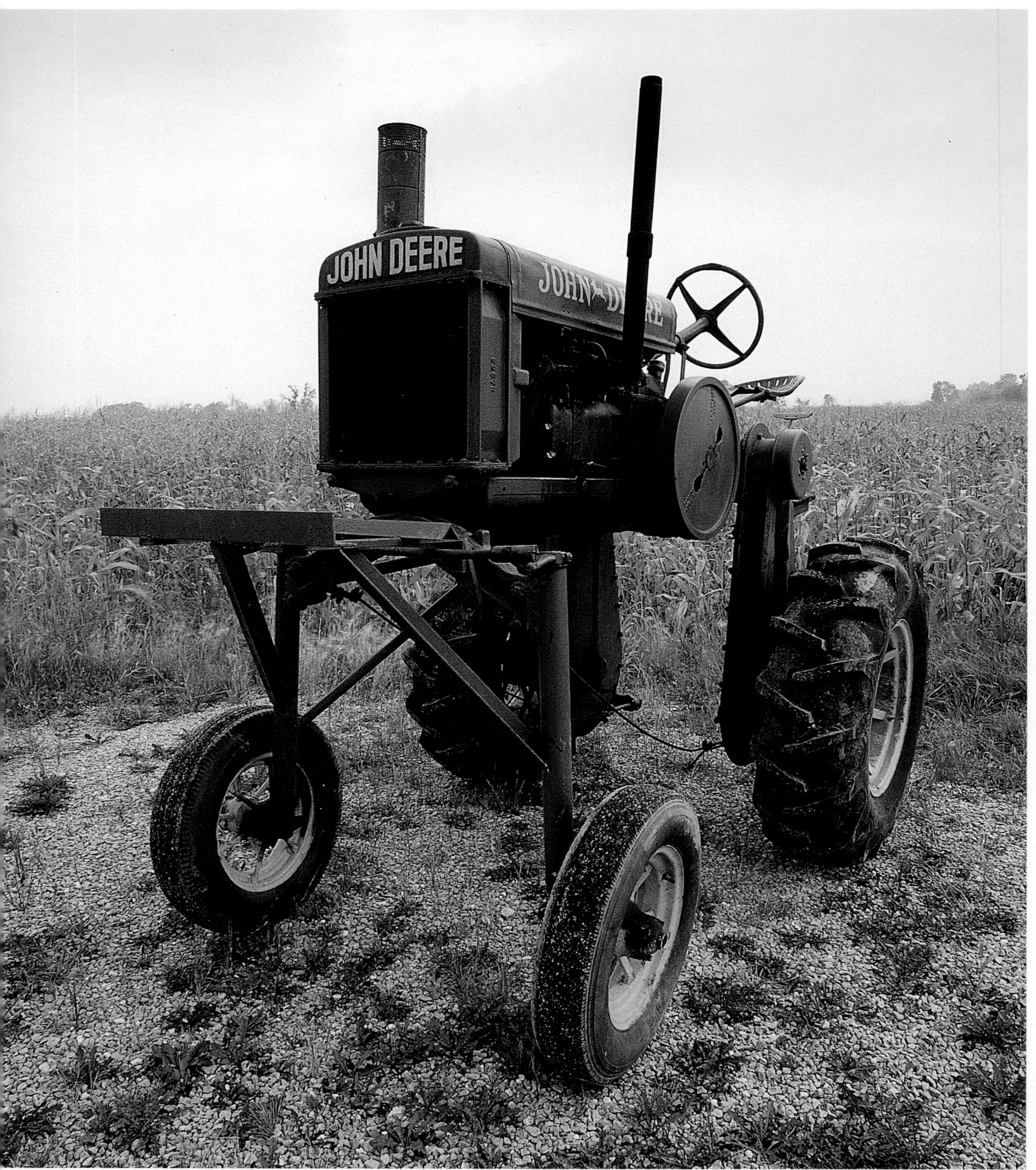

▲Each set of front and rear stilts was virtually custom made although only two standard heights were available, 4.5 and 6.0 ft. The row width could be specified although it was not adjustable. Heat-treated 2.5in diameter stub axles were welded on to the rear stilts, and Timken bearings were used in steel hubs. Standard wheels were used. This 1948 Model B is owned by Walter and Bruce Keller of Kaukauna, Wisconsin.

▸In order to spray, dust, or defoliate cotton, or to cultivate, fertilize, or to top corn, most manufacturers left the farmer too low even with their high-clearance or hi-crop models. But Tractor Stilts Company, Inc. of Omaha, Nebraska, had an answer. The company produced its first stilts in 1948 and manufactured them for any tractor make or model.

JOHN DEERE
JOHN DEERE

BE CAREFUL

◂*Live power-take-off was one of Cockshutt's claims to fame. This left the PTO shaft spinning independently of ground speed, enabling towed implements to continue their work even as the tractor might slow for the end of the row or stop altogether. Live—or independent—PTO did not originate with Cockshutt. It was first offered on Hart-Parr Model 18-36 tractors as early as 1926. PTO was first available on International Harvester Model 8-16 tractors introduced in 1918.*

▴*Gambles—Cockshutt—used an in-line vertical four-cylinder Buda gasoline engine. The engine measured 3.43x4.125in bore and stroke. The Buda produced 21.7hp on the drawbar and a peak of 30.3 belt pulley horsepower. Fuel economy was measured at 11.4 horsepower hours per gallon. Four forward gears offered top road speed of 10mph. The Model 30 weighed 3,609lb.*

◂◂*The Cockshutt Model 30 was the first Canadian-manufactured tractor to be tested at the University of Nebraska. It was sold in the U.S. under license by both Farmers Cooperatives as the Model E-3 and by the Gambles Department Store chain as its Farmcrest Model 30. On each of the U.S. versions, the Cockshutt embossing on the grille was left unpainted but still readily visible. This was the 1949 Gambles.*

Gambles FARMCREST
30

▲ *Raynard Schmidt of Vail, Iowa, restored and owns this Canadian-built row-crop. Cockshutt tractors were among the most stylish of the streamlined machines. The Brantford, Ontario firm (located near Toronto) used an architectural designer to design the machines. Cockshutt was eventually absorbed by Oliver and ultimately became part of the large White Farm Equipment family.*

▲*The frost of a late fall morning in western Iowa is a long way from the cotton fields of the south or west but as collectors recognize the unique engineering features of certain machines, one region's specialty becomes another's curiosity. The Type 314 low-cylinder cotton picker was mounted on a 1950 Model M. The entire assembly stood 150in tall (basket closed), 104in wide, and 208in long overall. The basket itself measured 72in tall, 104in wide, and 77in long.*

◄*Bob Pollock of Denison, Iowa, runs the hydraulics on his M to swing open the cotton bin and keep the entire system in working order. International production of the Farmall M ran from 1939 through 1952. In 1940, the tractor (without cotton picker) sold for $1,112. The four-cylinder IHC engine produced 34.4hp on the drawbar and 39.2 on the belt pulley. A three-plow tractor, more than two hundred thousand Model Ms were produced and thousands are still in use.*

▸ *The R.H. Sheppard Company of Hanover, Pennsylvania, began producing tractors in 1949 after years of making stationary diesel power units from 5.4 up to 100hp. The SD-3 was its middle of the line machine. The SD-2 and, after 1955, its SD-4, were offered as row-crop or standard tread machines. Early Sheppard tractors had reliability problems with the Detroit Timken Axle Company's rear ends. The SD-4 introduced Sheppard's own rear end, but their reputation was too badly damaged, and Sheppard quit producing tractors at the end of 1958.*

SD-3
SHEPPARD DIESEL

▲Sheppard's engine cylinders had a pre-combustion chamber that allowed very high compression—22:1. Despite this, the Sheppard was a very smooth-running engine. Before International Harvester offered its own diesel for the Farmall M, Sheppard produced a conversion kit. It used the internal pieces but in a block specifically manufactured to mate to the IHC engine mounts and flywheel/clutch assembly. Fuel economy was often quoted as a fifty-gallon drum of diesel plowed forty acres. This 1952 Sheppard is owned and still used by Ray Errett of Harlan, Iowa.

▸Oddly, while Sheppard used an outside vendor rear axle which caused reliability problems and earned a bad reputation, the company made its own fuel-injection system involving a gravity feed right to the plunger. The system had no booster pump. Sheppards were never tested at Nebraska. But the three-cylinder engine had 4.0x5.0in bore and stroke for a total capacity of 188.5ci. At 1,650rpm, the company reported 32 drawbar and pulley horsepower.

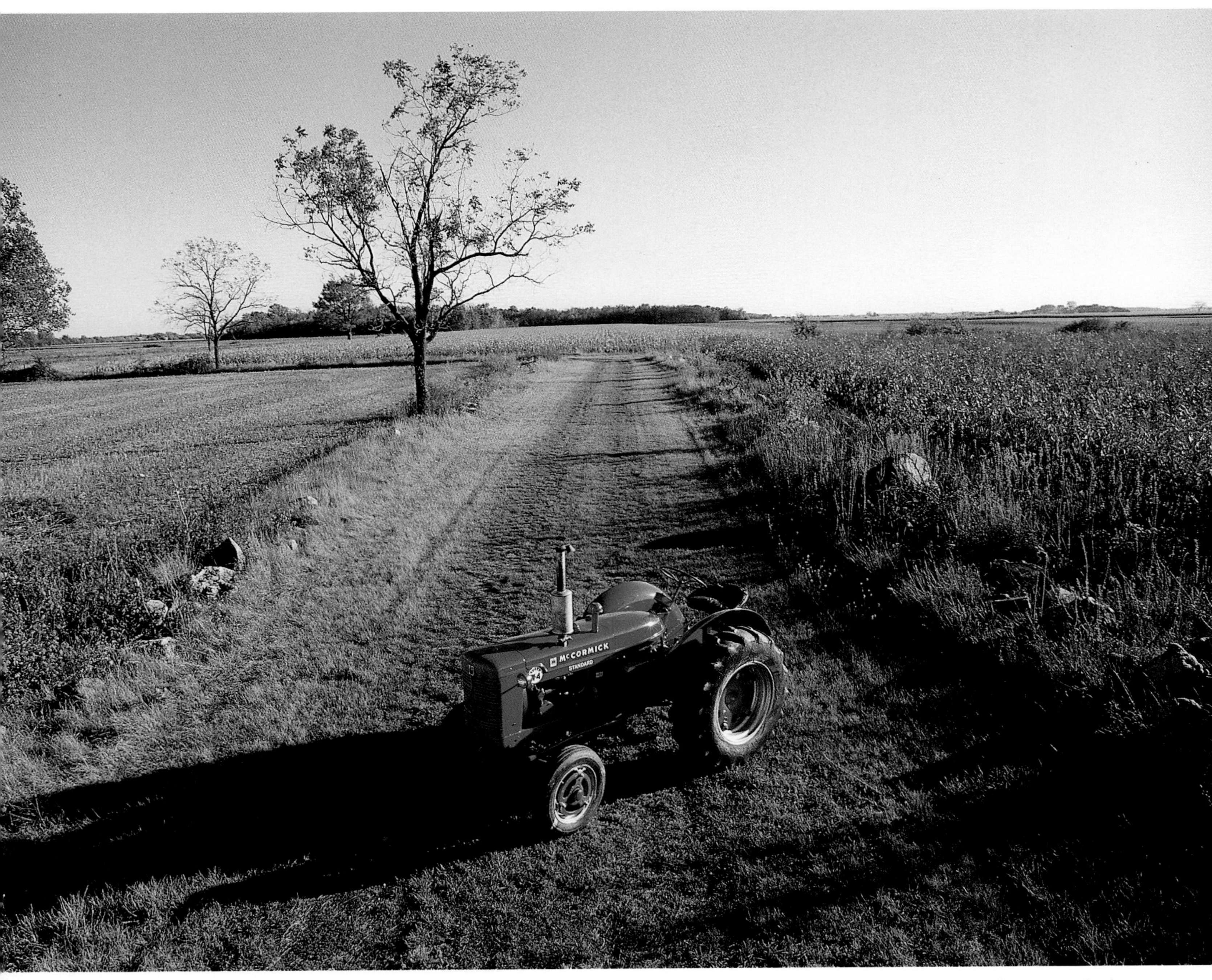

▲*The Super W-4 was rated as a three-plow tractor. Delivered on rubber tires, it weighed 3,915lb. On-board hydraulics were optional, as was the PTO, which was independent. The International Harvester-built transmission offered five-speeds forward and one reverse.*

▲*International's type C-164 engine measured 3.5x4.25in bore and stroke for total capacity of 164ci. Tested at the University of Nebraska in May 1953, the W-4 produced 23.1 hp on the drawbar and a maximum of 31.5hp on the belt pulley at 1,650rpm. Road gear offered a top speed of 15mph. Paul Brecheisen of Helena, Ohio, restored and owns this 1953 Super W-4.*

▸*International Harvester ended the thirteen-year production of its W-4 model in 1953, introducing the Super W-4 at the same time. This was a styled version of the W-4 with a new grille and some changes to the front frame for strength, stiffness, and implement attachment. The tractor measured 82in tall to the top of the stack, 65in wide, and 120in long overall (to the tip of the hitch), on a 67in wheelbase.*

▸▸*The Harris Manufacturing Company of Stockton, California, produced its Model 53 using an industrial Chrysler Model 8A in-line six-cylinder engine. Bore and stroke were 3.43x4.50in for total capacity of 250.6ci. At 2,000rpm, the Chrysler produced a maximum 44.5hp on its drawbar (it had no belt pulley but Harris rated brake horsepower at 62.) The Power Horse steered much like crawler tractors, with hand-operated wheel brakes slowing or stopping either side individually or both together. The Model 53 measured 78in tall, 75in wide, and 107in long. The Laird Welding and Manufacturing Model D-76 blade added 15in to the width and 16in to overall length. This 1954 tractor was owned by the late Tiny Blom of Manilla, Iowa.*

McCORMICK
STANDARD

HARRIS
WER-HORSE

▲*Oliver's smallest tractor was produced only during 1957 and 1958. Its manufacture was a kind of company hot potato, beginning at the Battle Creek, Michigan, plant and then moving to the South Bend, Indiana, facilities. Its replacement, the 440, was then produced at the Charles City, Iowa, plant where Hart-Parr tractors were first made.*

▸*The Super 44 was produced as an offset tractor designed primarily for commercial nurseries and gardens. The offset operating position permitted the tractor's compact dimensions and also allowed the operator greater visibility for cultivating. The tractor was 80in tall to the stack, 54in wide, and 118in overall. The engine was an in-line four-cylinder Continental gasoline, never tested at Nebraska. This 1958 Super 44 was owned by the late Tiny Blom of Manilla, Iowa.*

▲*Several—the number is not exactly known—prototypes were sent out for field testing. One tractor was held at the Waterloo factory for work moving equipment and raw materials around the yard. Records indicate the field prototypes were destroyed when they were returned to the factory. One story says the factory yard tractor dragged them off to the cutting torches. This is reported to be the yard prototype.*

◄*This was part of Deere & Co.'s first efforts with articulated four-wheel drive. The Model 8010 was produced only in a small series of prototypes to work out the bugs inherent in something so drastically—and dramatically—different from anything Deere had done before. Bruce Kellar swivels the 8010 in a corn field near home in Kaukauna, Wisconsin.*

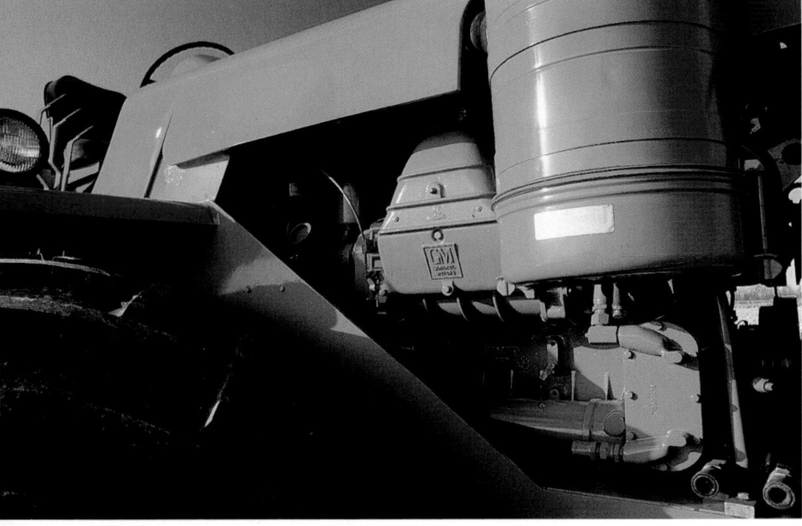

▲*It's large. The Model 8010 stands 99in to the top of the steering wheel, 96in wide and—on its 120in wheelbase—it stretches 238in in overall length. Its fuel capacity is 106 gallons. It weighs 26,450lb. Each of its four identical tires is 23.1x26in.*

◂*Power for the 8010 came from a six-cylinder two-cycle in-line GMC diesel fitted with a GMC supercharger. Bore and stroke were 4.25x5.00in, with a total capacity of 425ci. The compression ratio of the diesel engine was 17.0:1. Recommended engine operating speed was 2,100rpm which, in eighth gear would provide 18mph on the road. Drawbar pull was established by Deere at 20,000lb, from an estimated 150hp.*

▸▸*Deere would go on to produce huge articulated four-wheel drive tractors. However, Walter and Bruce Keller's Model 8010 prototype looks dated alongside a more contemporary Model 4850 equipped with Caster/Action MFWD (mechanical front-wheel drive). A year after the 8010 prototype, Deere introduced its New Generation of Power, with its own in-line four- and six-cylinder diesels. Within a short time, Deere and other manufacturers would add turbochargers and then intercoolers to produce nearly twice the horsepower of GMC's supercharged six.*

JOHN DEERE
4850

JOHN DEERE
8010
DIESEL

Index

Photo Index

Note that when several of the models listed consectutively had the same owner, the owner was listed after the last listing. The first two Allis-Chalmers models are an example. Both the Model E and Model UC are owned by Conrad Shoessler.

Subject Index